DIREKT!

Communicative Skills for GCSE and S-Grade German

Margaret Wightman

John Murray

Pupils' Book
ISBN 0 7195 4593 5
Teachers' Resource Book
ISBN 0 7195 4594 3
Cassettes (set of three)
ISBN 0 7195 4595 1

Author's note
This is the **Pupils' Book** for **Direkt**!, providing activities for individuals, pairs and groups to help students preparing for communicative examinations in German, such as GCSE and Scottish S-Grade. It is designed to be used with the cassette tapes containing the spoken material for the listening sections of each unit, and with the **Teachers' Resource Book**.

The **Teachers' Resource Book** contains a full introduction for teachers, photocopiable sheets of extra tasks (including exercises, games, jokes and puzzles), a complete assessment test with mark scheme, a continuous assessment chart, transcripts of the listening materials and selected answers. There is also advice for candidates on how to tackle the examination, under the title *Merke dir das!*

I should like to acknowledge the help and encouragement given to me by my publishers, and by Harold, Emma and Martin, my long-suffering family. Thanks also to the Müllers of Horst and Munich, the Blum family, Mathias Schmidt, Elfrieda Richter and countless other friends who, often unwittingly, have helped to prepare this book. **Direkt**! is in series with **En Direct**! by Jean-Claude Gilles, whose permission to use the original arrangement and format is gratefully acknowledged. A list of detailed acknowledgements appears on p.96.

M.W.

First published 1989
by John Murray (Publishers) Ltd
50 Albemarle Street, London
W1X 4BD

Printed and bound in Great Britain by
Butler & Tanner Ltd, Frome and London

British Library Cataloguing In
Publication Data

Wightman, Margaret
  Direkt: communicative skills for
  GCSE German.
  1. Great Britain. Secondary
  schools. Curriculum subjects:
  German language. Oral
  examination. Techniques
  I. Title
  438

ISBN 0-7195-4593-5

CONTENTS

1 BASIC Listening

Personal background, daily routine, meeting people

1 Your new exchange partner has made a tape introducing herself and her family. The tape is in sections. You will hear each section twice. Listen carefully, then answer the questions below.

Section 1

How old is your partner?

Section 2

When is her birthday?

Section 3

Which class is she in at school?

Section 4

How many brothers and sisters does she have?

Section 5

Who is the youngest in the family?

Section 6

What does her father do for a living?

Section 7

Is her house old or new?

Section 8

Who is Peterchen?

2 You will hear a boy asking a girl to come to a disco. You will hear the conversation twice.

1 Why can't she come?

2 What pets does the boy have?

3 You will hear a girl phoning home. You will hear the message twice.

1 What time will the girl be home?

2 Why will she be late?

4 On the radio the police are appealing for information about a child missing from the town where you are staying. The tape is in sections. You will hear each section twice. Copy and complete the description of the child.

Section 1	Section 2
Boy or Girl?	Height
Age	Hair colour
Clothing	Eye colour
Shoes	

1 An English teenager is discussing the evening meal with her German friend. The tape is in sections. You will hear each section twice. Listen carefully and then answer the questions below.

Section 1

1 What kind of evening meal could you expect in this household?

2 List five things they might eat.

Section 2

3 What would the visitor have liked?

4 What does this family never eat in the evening?

5 What might they occasionally have for breakfast?

Section 3

6 How many courses does the English family have in the evening?

7 Why don't they eat at a fixed time?

2 Your penfriend's father is talking to a visitor who has just moved into a new house. Which of the following does the new house have? You will hear the conversation twice.

a) breakfast room
b) living room
c) dining room
d) kitchen
e) bedrooms
f) bathroom
g) study
h) cellar
i) boiler room
j) laundry room
k) wine store
l) garden

3 Your visit to West Germany coincides with a flood of refugees arriving from eastern bloc countries. Many had to leave everything behind.

i) One of the new arrivals is being interviewed on the radio. The tape is in sections. You will hear each section twice.

Section 1

1 Which country has this man left?

2 Who came with him?

Section 2

3 How old was the youngest person in the group?

4 How did they travel to Germany?

Section 3

5 When did they speak German at home?

6 Do his children also speak German?

ii) Charity workers provide the refugees with basic essentials. An interview with two charity workers follows. You will hear each section twice.

Section 4

1 List four items of clothing that are provided.

2 What advice do the men get from their wives?

Section 5

3 What do the refugees think about the clothing they are given?

4 What special problem is there with the clothes being distributed at the moment?

1 BASIC Speaking

1 It's your first morning in Germany. Your exchange partner has gone to school. You come downstairs to find Frau Arendt in the kitchen. Work in pairs, taking turns to play each role.

FRAU ARENDT	YOU
Ah! Guten Morgen!	Greet her.
Hast du gut geschlafen?	Say yes, thanks.
Hast du Hunger?	Reply.
Trinkst du gern eine Tasse Tee?	Say please, with milk.
Ich trinke auch eine Tasse.	Ask if you can help.
Ja, gerne.	

2 You are on a school exchange during term time, so you're attending a German school. The class teacher is asking you about yourself. Work in pairs, taking turns to play each role.

TEACHER	YOU
Ask the visitor if he/she speaks German.	Reply.
Ask what he/she is called.	Reply.
Ask where he/she is from.	Reply.
Ask how long he/she has been learning German.	Reply.
Ask if he/she has any brothers and sisters.	Reply.
Ask if he/she is still at school.	Reply.
Ask where he/she is staying.	Reply.

3 You're getting to know your friend's exchange partner. Work in pairs, taking turns to play each role.

FRIEND 1	FRIEND 2
Ask if he/she has any pets.	Say yes, a little dog.
Say you've also got a dog. Ask if he/she has a hobby.	Say you play guitar. Ask if he/she plays an instrument.
Say no, but you play table tennis.	Say you hate sport!
Ask if he/she likes pop music.	Say quite, but also classical.
Ask if he/she would like an ice cream.	Say no thanks, you don't like it.

4 A German exchange pupil is showing you a photograph of his/her family. Use these questions and the photograph to make up a conversation. Work in pairs.

1 Wer steht ganz rechts?
2 Wie alt ist er?
3 Geht er noch zur Schule?
4 Wer hat das Bild gemacht?
5 Ist das Bild von diesem Jahr?
6 Wohnst du in dieser Stadt?
7 Gefällt es dir dort? Warum?

1 In the Goldberg Gymnasium the teacher is trying to involve the exchange pupils in the next geography lesson. She has asked you all to prepare and give a brief talk to the class about your home area. Work in threes; each take one of the following examples, adding more information if you can.

A You live in a suburb of a city in northern England – once was lots of industry – many unemployed – was dirty, now cleaner – new shops, theatre, museum – an interesting place – tourists come.

B You live near a village in Wales – father a farmer – farm in a valley – nearest town several miles away – your school is there – last bus home at 5 o'clock – like living on a farm – farmhouse over 300 years old.

C You live in a new town in southern England – everything modern except castle in town centre – industrial area has many small factories – easy to find a job – don't like the town, it's boring.

2 In town you witness a minor road accident involving a boy from your penfriend's class. You can't recall his name, so you have to describe him to your penfriend. What do you say? ▶

3 You are staying with an Austrian family. Grandfather speaks no English. He's asking you lots of questions, but he doesn't speak clearly. Work in pairs, taking turns to play each role.

OPA	YOU
Haben Sie eine große Wohnung?	Ask him to repeat the question.
Repeat it.	Reply.
Und haben Sie auch einen Garten?	Reply.
Wohnen Sie direkt in der Stadt?	Say you don't understand.
Wohnen Sie in der Stadtmitte?	Reply.
Sie sprechen aber ein gutes Deutsch! Lernen Sie Deutsch in der Schule?	Ask him to speak slowly, please!
Repeat your question more slowly.	Tell him how long you have been learning.
Sind Sie zum ersten Mal hier in Österreich?	Say no, you came last year.

1
BASIC
Reading

1 Read these announcements and answer the questions.

1 Why did Detlef's family put an announcement in the newspaper?

> Lieber Detlef,
> am 18. wirst Du
>
> **18**
>
> Herzlichen Glückwunsch zum Geburtstag.
> *Mutti, Klaus, Thomas, Holger und Michael*

2 What happened on November 18th, 1987? ▼

> Wir sind verlobt.
> Irmgard Müller
> &
> Helmut Jordan
>
> 18. Nov. 1987   in Lollar

4 What has happened to Frau Grefe? ▼

> Am 8. Oktober 1987 ist unsere liebe Tante
>
> ## Frau Dorothea Grefe
>
> gestorben.
>
> In stiller Trauer:
> **Dr. Rainer Fritsch**
> **Dr. Gisela Fritsch** geb. Wurm
> **mit Marie-Christine und Andreas**
>
> Die Beisetzung ist am 16. Oktober erfolgt.

3 What are the Schröders announcing?
▼

> Wir haben am
> 15. Oktober 1987 geheiratet
>
> *Beate Schröder*
> geb. Heitmüller
> *Uwe Schröder*
>
> 3016 Seelze 4, Gümmerdamm 17

5 Who is Lothar Müller?
▼

> LOTHAR
> 20.5.1988
>
> UNSER ZWEITER JUNGE IST ANGEKOMMEN
>
> SUSANA MÜLLER GEB. SULCEUKO
> DIPL.-ING. ULFRID MÜLLER
>
> GODSHORN ÜBER HANNOVER
> BIRKENALLEE 32

> Wir freuen uns ganz herzlich über die Geburt unserer Tochter
>
> Lisa Sophie
> 10. Oktober 1987
>
> *Susanne und*
> *Dr. med. dent. D. Oppermann*
>
> 3000 Hannover 81, Brandestraße 11

 6 Why will the Oppermanns remember October 19th, 1987?

2
1 For which two events is Mechthild sending greetings?

2 What has arrived?

3 What does she plan to do soon?

10.12.86

Liebe Margaret,
lieber Harold,
liebe Emma,
lieber Martin,
Euch wünschen wir ein recht
frohes, gesundes Weihnachtsfest
und ein gutes, gesegnetes
neues Jahr. Eure 3 Päckchen
sind gut angekommen
Heute nur ganz kurz.
Viele Grüße von uns allen.
Ein Brief folgt später.
Eure Mechthild + Familie

3 In Mirja's last letter she described her bedroom to you:

1 What advantages does Mirja's bed have?

2 Why does she have such a lot of shelves?

3 What are on the window sill?

4 Where could she do her homework?

▼

Bei mir ist es, daß mein Zimmer sehr klein
ist. Meine Eltern haben mir ein Bett gekauft, das ich
tagsüber als Sofa gebrauchen kann. Dann habe
ich viele Regale an den Wänden, in denen meine
vielen Bücher stehen. Meine Fensterbank ist
ganz voll von Blumen, außerdem habe ich noch
zwei Blumenampeln. Das wichtigste in meinem
Schlafzimmer ist aber natürlich mein Schreibtisch.

1 HIGHER
Reading

1 Your exchange partner and his/her family are moving to the house described in this advert. Your family is curious to know what the advert says.

1 What type of house is it?

2 When was it built?

3 Does it have a garden?

4 Is it on a main road?

5 They have a sauna! Where is it?

6 Are they buying or renting?

> **Erlangen:** Einfamilienhaus, Baujahr 84 zu verkaufen. 180 m² Wohnfläche, 6 Zimmer, Küche, Bad/WC, Diele, Keller (Sauna, Hobbyraum, Waschküche), Zentralheizung, 2 Garagen, Terrasse, 250 m² Garten, sonnige Lage, kein Verkehr. 750 000. Tel 0852 35 36.

2 Easter is an important celebration in Siggi's family. This is her description of the long Easter weekend:

Für uns Kinder ist es eine wunderschöne Zeit. Ostern beginnt für uns schon am Gründonnerstag. Zum Mittagessen gibt es das erste Festmahl. Zum Kaffeetrinken essen wir eine schöne Torte. Abends um 18.00 Uhr gehen wir dann in die Kirche. Aber Karfreitag ist noch schöner. Morgens um 10.00 Uhr ist Gottesdienst. Um 13.00 Uhr wird Mittag gegessen. Dann kommt ein toller Film im Fernsehen; danach wird Kaffee getrunken.

Karsamstag ist leider für uns Kinder nur ein Tag voller Arbeit. Es müssen nämlich die Eier für Ostersonntag gefärbt werden, damit es schön bunt aussieht.

Am Ostersonntag stehen dann die bunten Eier auf dem Frühstückstisch. Um 10.00 Uhr fängt der Kindergottesdienst in der Kirche an. Die Helfer haben für jeden von uns Kindern ein kleines Osterei aus Schokolade. Während wir in der Kirche sind, versteckt unsere Mama noch viele Eier. Wir müssen sie also erst noch suchen, bevor wir anfangen können, sie zu essen. Es macht viel Spaß! Danach kommt das Festmahl. Ein schöner Braten und danach ein schöner Nachtisch. Am Nachmittag gibt es dann tolle Torten und Kuchen.

1 On which day of the week do the Easter celebrations begin?

2 What happens at 10 am on Good Friday?

3 How does the family spend Good Friday afternoon?

4 What keeps the children occupied on Easter Saturday?

5 What do the children receive in church on Sunday?

6 What is such good fun between church and lunch on Easter Sunday?

7 List four things that are eaten on Easter Sunday.

8 Would you say that Siggi enjoys eating?

3 In *ZECHE* magazine you find this article about the disc-jockey John Peel.

Backstage:
John Peel (DJ)

Er macht seit nunmehr 27 Jahren Radio, ist verheiratet, hat vier Kinder und lebt mit seiner Familie weit außerhalb Londons auf dem Land. Begonnen hat er seine Karriere bei einer lokalen Radiostation in Dallas, Texas und diversen Sendern an der US-amerikanischen Westküste. Heute macht er dreimal in der Woche Programm bei der BBC, Montags bis Mittwochs bei der BBC, Montags bis Mittwochs jeweils von 22.00–24.00 Uhr, ist einmal wöchentlich bei uns im BFBS zu hören (Freitags von 22.00–24.00 Uhr) und wöchentlich Freitags von 22.00–24.00 Uhr auch bei Radio Bremen 4 aktiv. Sein Programm ist anders als alle anderen und die Popszene wäre ohne ihn erheblich langweiliger. Ab Oktober wird er in der ZECHE Bands seiner Wahl vorstellen.

Frage: Wieviele Platten hast Du im Laufe der Jahre gesammelt?
PEEL: Es sind bis jetzt etwa 19,000 LPs und eine Vielzahl von Singles, von denen ich nicht weiß, wieviele es sind.

Frage: Nach welchen Gesichtspunkten wählst Du die Platten für Deine Programme aus?
PEEL: Ganz einfach: ich spiele die Platten, die mir gefallen. Es sind Sachen, die mir gefallen und von denen ich meine, sie sollten im Radio gespielt werden.

Frage: Welchen Hinweis würdest Du Deinen Kolleginnen und Kollegen in den Sendern geben?
PEEL: Ich glaube, die DJs, insbesondere in England, sollten aufhören, soviel leeres, eigensüchtiges Geschwätz zu verbreiten und sich mehr auf die Musik konzentrieren.

BFBS = British Forces Broadcasting Service.

4 Your penfriend Birgit is writing to tell you about her Tuesdays:

1 What time does the first lesson begin on Tuesdays?

2 Why is this particular Tuesday different?

3 What was Birgit able to do this morning?

4 What does Birgit's mother do after lunch?

5 What happens between 3 and 4 pm?

6 When do Birgit and her mother have coffee?

7 Give two things which Birgit might do after the evening meal.

8 Why does she go to bed so early?

True or false?

a) John Peel is divorced.

b) He lives near London.

c) He used to work in America.

d) He broadcasts every weekday evening.

e) His programmes are just like all the other music programmes.

f) He will be writing articles about pop music for the magazine.

g) He doesn't know exactly how many records he possesses.

h) He wouldn't dream of giving any advice to fellow DJs.

Normalerweise muß ich am Dienstag zur ersten Stunde in die Schule. Meine Englischlehrerin ist aber krank, und so fällt bei mir die erste Stunde aus. Dadurch mußte ich heute nicht schon um 8.00 Uhr in der Schule sein, sondern erst um 8.50 Uhr. Ein Glück! So konnte ich länger schlafen!

Dienstags habe ich immer um 13.30 Uhr Schulschluß. Bis ich zu Hause bin, ist es 14.00 Uhr. Meine Mutter und ich essen schnell Mittag, weil meine Mutter arbeiten geht. Sie macht 1½ Stunden Hausaufgabenhilfe bei einem Nachbarskind. Ich fange an, Hausaufgaben zu machen, aber um 15.00 Uhr kommt meine Klavierschülerin. Ich gebe ihr eine Stunde in der Woche Unterricht. Wenn meine Mutter von der Arbeit kommt, trinken wir zusammen Kaffee.

In der Regel kommt mein Vater um 19.00 Uhr nach Hause. Wir essen dann Abendbrot und unterhalten uns ein bißchen. Wenn es was schönes im Fernsehen gibt, gucken wir es uns manchmal an. Sonst mache ich schon wieder Hausaufgaben. Um 21.30 Uhr fange ich normalerweise an, ins Bett zu gehen, weil ich mittwochs die erste Stunde habe, und ich um 6.30 Uhr aufstehen muß.

1 BASIC Writing

1 Your exchange partner's birthday falls soon after you return home from staying with the family. Write an appropriate birthday greeting on the card you are sending – and don't forget to say a big thank you for a fabulous holiday.

2 Your penfriend's mother has gone to the shops and your penfriend is having a guitar lesson. Shaun and Lisa, who are staying across the road, ask you to go for a walk in the park. They say they will be back in about an hour. Leave a note in German saying:

- where you have gone
- who you are with
- when you will be back.

3 Whilst your friend is at school his/her mother is called away. She tells you quickly what needs to be done. After she has left, you note down in German what she said:

- buy bread and cakes
- lunch in fridge
- wash up
- tidy bedroom
- make coffee at 4.30.

4 Your teacher has just handed you this sheet with details of your new penfriend. Write your first letter to her, introducing yourself and telling her about your family, house, pets and hobbies. Try to find out the same kind of information from her.

```
Katrin Wolff
Panoramaweg 23
7032 Sindelfingen
16 Jahre
```

1 Soon you'll be travelling to stay with the Schwarz family. Write to them giving details of your travel arrangements. Tell them how to recognise you and say how much you are looking forward to your stay. The notes below will help.

Wed Aug 5th – 7.15 ferry Dover – Ostende

Intercity train Ostende – Cologne; arr. Cologne 4.35 pm.
Meet them on platform?
MUST enclose photo with my new glasses!

Travelling in jeans + navy sweater; will have large red rucksack

2 Write a letter of about 100 words in German to your penfriend. Describe what happened on your sister's eighth birthday.

– Thank the family for the felt-tips they sent.

– Say what other presents she received – most important of all the black kitten your grandmother gave her.

– Tell your friend about her party; say why you had to organise and run it, who baked the cake, who came to help you on the day, what food you gave them, etc.

– Describe something that did not go according to plan.

– Ask what your friend will be doing on his/her birthday.

3 Last summer your neighbours exchanged homes with a family from your German twin town. Your parents would like to do the same next summer. They have asked you to write an advertisement describing your home to send to the twin town's newspaper. These are the details:

– it is in a quiet road near the centre of town, not far from the station

– about 10 minutes from the beach

– 3 bedrooms, modern kitchen, bath-room, large living room, garage, small garden with sunny patio

– would like to exchange for a similar house during last two weeks in July.

2 BASIC Listening

School and school exchanges

1 You will hear a man asking a young boy about school. The tape is in sections. You will hear each section twice.

Section 1

When will he begin to learn English?

Section 2

Where will the boy be going?

2 Ulrike is introducing a visitor to her friends. Listen to their conversation carefully and then answer the questions. You will hear each section twice.

Section 1

Who is Louise?

Section 2

How long has Louise been in Germany?

How long is she staying?

Section 3

When does the return part of the exchange begin?

How many pupils are taking part in the exchange?

Section 4

What doesn't Louise like about her visit so far?

3 You have just arrived at the house where you are going to stay in Germany. Your penfriend's mother is showing you round. You will hear each section of the tape twice.

Section 1

What are you being shown?

Section 2

Where is the toilet?

Section 3

What time do they usually get up?

Section 4

What is your friend's mother asking you?

Section 5

What are you being offered?

Section 6

When is lunch?

Section 7

What chore are you asked to do?

4 You will hear a mother talking to a young child. Listen carefully and then answer the questions. You will hear each section of the tape twice.

Section 1

What does she want him to do?

Section 2

Which subjects does he mention?

5 A group of German pupils is on an exchange visit to your school. Your German teacher is asking them what subjects they like. The recording is in sections. You will hear each section twice.

Section 1

1 Which year is Manuela in?

2 Which subjects does she enjoy?

Section 2

3 Which is Elke's favourite subject?

4 What does she not like?

Section 3

5 What subjects does Peter prefer?

6 Which ones don't interest him at all?

Section 4

7 What does Markus enjoy?

8 What does he think of other subjects?

1 You will hear a boy phoning a children's helpline. You will hear the conversation twice.

1 How does the boy feel?

2 How did the boy find out what mark he got in German?

3 Explain his father's reaction to the result.

4 Which subject has he done well in?

2 You are visiting Germany during term time. Your exchange partner is not in school today, so you have to note down the details of the class's annual outing. Copy the headings into your exercise book before the tape begins. The tape is in sections. You will hear each section twice.

> **KLASSENFAHRT**
>
> Day?
>
> Time to meet?
>
> Meeting place?
>
> Clothing?
> Anything else to take?
>
> Back at?

3 The teachers leading your exchange visit are being interviewed at the official reception. Listen carefully, then answer the questions below. You will hear each section twice.

Section 1

1 What has happened this year to the numbers taking part in the exchange?

2 Which country always shows the greater level of interest?

3 What could explain this fact?

Section 2

4 When do the British pupils visit Germany?

5 How do they travel?

6 Why do they travel this way?

7 Where does the British party come from?

Section 3

8 What excursions are arranged for the British pupils?

9 Where are the British pupils staying?

10 When are they returning home?

2
BASIC
Speaking

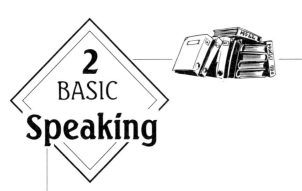

1 Work in pairs. Take turns to ask and answer these questions:

1 Wie kommst du zur Schule?

2 Wann beginnt die erste Stunde?

3 Wie lange dauert die kleine Pause?

4 Wo ißt du zu Mittag?

5 Welche Sportarten gibt es an deiner Schule?

6 Besuchst du ein Gymnasium?

7 Wieviele Fächer hast du?

8 Welche Fächer hast du heute?

9 Seit wann lernst du Deutsch?

10 Welche Clubs gibt es an deiner Schule?

2 You're discussing your favourite subjects with a German friend. Work in pairs. Take turns to play each part.

YOU	FRIEND
Ask what your friend's favourite subject is.	Answer. Ask if your friend likes it.
Say no, not at all. Your favourite subject is . . .	Say you think that is boring.
Ask if your friend is good at . . .	Say no. Ask your friend the same.
Say not specially, you find it hard.	Say you do too!

3 On holiday your family has met some Germans. They are keen to know about British schools. Using this timetable (or one of your own) tell them how you spend a typical day. Work in groups of 3–5.

▶

WEDNESDAY

8.50 – 9.00 Registration/tutorial

9.00 – 9.45 French

9.45 – 10.30 Chemistry

10.30 – 10.45 BREAK

10.45 – 11.30 History

11.30 – 12.15 English

12.15 – 1.15 LUNCH

1.15 – 2.45 P.E.

2.45 – 3.30 Maths

1 Anne Blum, aged 16, attends a Gymnasium in Erlangen. Compare her timetable with your own. Work in pairs, one answering the questions on the left, the other those on the right. Answer alternately.

Montag	Dienstag	Mittwoch	Donnerstag	Freitag	Samstag
Physik	Deutsch	Geschichte	Französisch	Französisch	
Chemie	Englisch	Physik	Religion	Englisch	
Musik	Religion	Deutsch	Zeichnen	Erdkunde	
Wirtschaft	Mathe	Englisch	Mathe	Biologie	
Geschichte	Französisch	Sport	Mathe	Mathe	
Deutsch	Biologie	Sport	Chemie		
	Chemie-Übung				
	Physik-Übung				

STUDENT 1

Wieviele Fächer hat Anne?

Wieviele Stunden hat sie in der Woche?

Wieviele Stunden hat Anne pro Tag?

In welchen Fächern gibt es Doppelstunden?

Welche Fremdsprachen lernt Anne?

Welche naturwissenschaftliche Fächer hat Anne?

Wieviele Stunden Mathe hat Anne?

Wieviele Stunden Deutsch hat sie?

Wieviele Stunden Sport hat Anne?

Welche Fächer gibt es nicht bei euch?

Eine Schulstunde dauert 45 Minuten; wer sitzt länger auf der Schulbank, Anne oder du?

STUDENT 2

Hast du mehr Fächer?

Wieviele hast du?

Wieviele hast du? Jeden Tag?

Wie ist es bei dir in der Schule?

Und du?

Und welche hast du?

Hast du genau so viele?

Wieviele Stunden Englisch hast du?

Und du?

Welche Fächer gibt es nicht in Deutschland?

2 Beantworten Sie diese Fragen:

1 Fangen deutsche Schulen auch um neun Uhr an?

2 Was ist in Deutschland eine Arbeit?

3 Welche Noten gibt es in Deutschland?

4 Was ist das Abitur?

5 Was passiert, wenn man in der Schule sitzenbleibt?

6 Beschreiben Sie Ihre Schule.

7 Was sind bei Ihnen in der Schule die Pflichtfächer?

8 Was machen Sie in den Pausen?

9 Was passiert, wenn ein Lehrer krank ist?

10 Erklären Sie, warum Sie (nicht) gern zur Schule gehen.

2 BASIC Reading

1 Your exchange partner's youngest brother is six. He received this card in the post today from his grandmother. What is happening?

Alles Gute zum Schul-Anfang.

MILKA. Die zarteste Versuchung, seit es Schokolade gibt.

2
1 Which foreign languages does Max learn?

2 How many science lessons does he have altogether?

3 Does he have both history and geography?

4 Which day do they have art?

5 What is the first lesson of the week?

Montag	Dienstag	Mittwoch	Donnerstag	Freitag	Samstag
WIRTSCHAFT	Deutsch	FRANZÖSISCH	ENGL.	FRANZ.	
ENGLISCH	MATHE.	ENGLISCH	Geschichte	BIOLOGIE	
RELI.	MATHE.	CHEMIE	Religion	Sport	
MATHE.	ENGLISCH	Geschichte	Deutsch	Sport	
Physik	ZEICHNEN	BIOLOGIE	Chemie	Sozialkunde	
DEUTSCH	FRANZ.		MATHE	Physik	
	Chemie				

Schneider Schulfüller

griffig

Name **MAX HIRSCH** Klasse **R2FR** Schuljahr **9**

3 Read this girl's account of games lessons, then answer the questions.

1 How often do they have games lessons?

2 How popular is sport?

3 What difference is there between the two sports halls?

4 What activities is the class doing at the moment in games lessons?

5 What happens at the end of the lesson?

6 What is planned for games lessons in the next few months?

Unsere Sportstunden haben wir bisher leider
so verteilt gehabt, daß wir zweimal in der
Woche eine 3/4 Stunde hatten. Da wir meistens
keine Lust zum Sport haben, bummeln
wir immer beim Ausziehen.
In meiner Schule gibt es eine große und
eine kleine Turnhalle. Wir haben abwechselnd
in der großen und in der kleinen Halle
Sport. Mit unserer Lehrerin haben wir
abgemacht, daß wir in der einen Stunde
ein Spiel machen und in der anderen
Stunde turnen. Als Spiel machen wir
im Augenblick Basketball. Wenn die
Stunde zu Ende ist, duschen wir als
erstes und kommen natürlich zu spät
zum Unterricht. Im nächsten Schulhalbjahr
werden wir 2 Stunden Schwimmen haben.
Wir freuen uns schon darauf!

1 Your German penfriend Tina has sent you this cutting from her local paper. Tina has an American girl staying with her at the moment.

1 How long is she staying?

2 Why are they holding a barbecue at the beginning of the exchange visit?

3 What new experience awaits the Americans from Thursday?

4 What is happening to the forest near Goslar?

5 How long will the Americans stay in Berlin?

6 Is the visit to Berlin meant to be purely for pleasure?

7 What is happening on the 24th?

8 Why should Tina and the other German exchange partners be feeling excited?

23 amerikanische Austauschschüler erwartet ein volles Programm

BERENBOSTEL(r). Der neunte, inzwischen schon traditionsreiche deutsch-amerikanische Schüleraustausch zwischen dem Gymnasium Berenbostel (GB) und den North Allegheny High Schools (NA) in Pittsburgh, Pennsylvania, hat begonnen.

Am letzten Montag wurden 23 amerikanische Schülerinnen und Schüler sowie drei Begleitpersonen unter Leitung von Jeff Maltz von ihren Garbsener Gastgebern empfangen. Bis zum 25. August werden sie nun ein interessantes und abwechslungsreiches Besuchsprogramm absolvieren, das ihnen Oberstudienrat Manfred Schröder zusammengestellt hat.

Dieses beginnt mit einer gemeinsamen Wanderung zum Kennenlernen durch das Steinhuder Moor sowie einer Fahrt nach Hagenburg, wo mit einem zünftigen Grillfest von den Sommerferien Abschied genommen wird.

Ab Donnerstag werden dann die amerikanischen Gäste Gelegenheit haben, den Schulalltag ihrer deutschen „Leidensgenossen" kennenzulernen, sofern dieser für sie nicht durch etwas Interessanteres unterbrochen wird, z. B. den Empfang durch den Bürgermeister der Stadt Garbsen im Bürgerhaus Havelse.

Zwei Höhepunkte des Aufenthaltes werden sicherlich die ganztägige Harzfahrt und die viertägige Berlinfahrt sein. Während das Bergmuseum und die Mineraliensammlung in Clausthal-Zellerfeld, Eindrücke vom mittelalterlichen Goslar, dem Waldsterben und der deutsch-deutschen Grenze nachhaltige Erlebnisse sein werden, so wird wahrscheinlich die größte deutsche Stadt, Berlin, noch stärker die Amerikaner berühren. Eine Stadtrundfahrt, diverse Informationsveranstaltungen zur politischen, wirtschaftlichen und kulturellen Situation der Stadt, West wie Ost, ein Besuch im größten deutschen Verlagshaus, das Checkpoint-Charlie-Museum, die Mutivisionsshow im Europa-Center und ein ganzer Tag in Ostberlin werden Stationen dieser Fahrt sein.

Natürlich wird neben dem offiziellen Besuchsprogramm in den drei Wochen auch viel Zeit für unterhaltsame Initiativen sein.

Aber auch manch private Fete und manch ein interessanter Familienausflug in die nähere Umgebung Garbsens oder weitere Umgebung wird stattfinden, bevor sich alle am 24. zum Abschiedsabend treffen und am darauffolgenden Morgen Abschied voneinander nehmen werden.

Für 22 Berenbosteler Gymnasiasten wird die Trennung aber nur gut drei Wochen betragen, denn dann heißt es für sie: Ab nach Amerika!

2 BASIC Writing

1 Write a note to your penfriend to say:

– Thank you for the invitation, but you can't come to stay from February 5th to 12th.

– Your exams begin on the 4th and they are very important.

– You hope you will get good marks, but you are not very good at most subjects.

– Wish your friend a happy Christmas.

2 Study the pictures below, then tell the story in German.

Tübingen, den 11. November

Liebe Lisa!

Ich freue mich, daß ich Deine Brieffreundin werden darf. Ich weiß, daß Du schon 16 Jahre alt bist. Gehst Du noch zur Schule? In welcher Klasse bist Du? Schickst Du mir ein Bild von Dir? Ich bin in der 10. Klasse. Nächstes Jahr komme ich hoffentlich in die Oberstufe. Unser Englischlehrer hat uns erzählt, daß die Schule bei Euch erst um 9.00 Uhr losgeht. Ihr habt vielleicht Glück! Ich muß schon um 6.15 Uhr aufstehen, denn ich fahre fast 1 Stunde mit dem Bus bis zur Schule. Stimmt es auch, daß Ihr alle eine Uniform tragen müßt? Komisch! Kommst Du in allen Fächern genausogut mit? Ich bekomme in Physik immer schlechte Noten. Das klappt einfach nicht bei mir! In der vorletzten Arbeit schrieb ich sogar eine Fünf. Da haben meine Eltern vielleicht geschimpft! Seit der Zeit bekomme ich in Physik Nachhilfeunterricht.

Ich freue mich sehr auf Deinen ersten Brief!

Schöne Grüße, auch an Deine Eltern — hast Du auch Geschwister?

Deine Martina

1 This is the first letter you have received from your new penfriend. Read it carefully, then write a reply in German of about 100 words.

2 Study the pictures below, then tell the story in German.

3 BASIC Listening

Getting about

1 You're at the station, waiting for your train home. There is a steady stream of enquiries at the information desk on platform 3. The tape was made in sections. You will hear each section twice.

Section 1

What does the woman want to know?

What does the man tell her?

Section 2

What is the man asking about the journey to Bentheim?

What is the reply?

Section 3

This woman is going to Amsterdam. When can she leave?

What time should she arrive?

Section 4

What is about to happen on platform 3?

2 A group of friends is deciding where to meet. Are they meeting

a) at the bus stop?

b) in a snack bar?

c) at a cake shop?

d) in an ice-cream parlour?

3 ### Section 1

A boy is booking rail tickets. You will hear the dialogue twice.

– How many tickets does he ask for?

– Does he ask for singles or returns?

– What class is he travelling?

Section 2

A woman is buying petrol. You will hear the conversation twice.

– How much petrol does she ask for?

– What grade does she need?

4 A girl is being told how to get a tram ticket. Listen carefully and then answer the questions below. You will hear each section twice.

Section 1

Where should she get the ticket from?

Section 2

What must she do with the ticket?

5 You will hear three people asking for directions. The sketch map shows you where they are standing. The recording is in three sections. You will hear each section twice. Listen carefully and then answer the questions.

Section 1

1 Where does the woman want to go?

2 Which building is it on the map?

Section 2

3 Where does the woman want to go?

4 Which building is it on the map?

5 How long will it take her to get there?

Section 3

6 Which place is the man looking for?

7 Which building is it on the map?

8 What is it next door to?

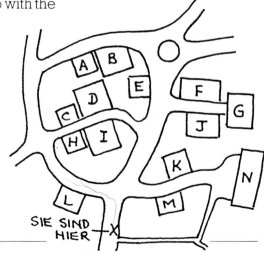

SIE SIND HIER

1 A woman is in the Verkehrsamt asking how to get to her hotel. Listen to the tape, which is in two sections, then answer the questions below. You will hear each section twice.

Section 1

Why can the woman not take the most direct route?

Section 2

Where should she turn right?

What landmark will help her find the hotel?

2 A man is giving his daughter directions to her new music teacher's home. You will hear his instructions twice.

  1 What transport will she use first?

  2 What must she do when she reaches the main station?

  3 When she is in the Sommerstraße, how will the girl find the house she is looking for?

3 You are waiting to catch the train to the Hook of Holland when you hear this announcement.

  – Is your train arriving now, or must you still wait a while?

  – What time will the train depart?

You will hear the announcement twice.

4 You are driving along the motorway A7 from Kassel to Hamburg (see sketch map). On the way you hear several road traffic bulletins on the car radio. You will hear each of them twice.

Bulletin 1

  1 What general warning is given to motorists?

  2 What has happened between Göttingen and Hanover?

  3 Which side of the motorway is affected?

Bulletin 2

  4 What has caused the problem north of Göttingen?

  5 What additional hazard is there at the scene?

Bulletin 3

  6 What is wrong between Mellendorf and Schwarmstedt?

  7 What are motorists recommended to do?

Bulletin 4

  8 What is happening to traffic approaching the Elbe Tunnel?

3 BASIC Speaking

1 Work in pairs, taking turns to play each part. One of you is a resident in a German town, the other is a visitor.

VISITOR	RESIDENT
Ask a passer-by where the tourist office is.	Say it is in the town hall.
Ask where that is.	Say it is left here, then straight on.
Ask if it is far.	Say no, five or six minutes.
Thank him/her and say goodbye.	Say goodbye.

2 One of you is a railway clerk, the other is a traveller.

CLERK	TRAVELLER
Guten Morgen.	Greet the clerk and ask for two tickets to Cologne, second class.
Einfach oder hin und zurück?	Answer the question.

Now book the tickets shown in this table.

Number	Class	Destination	> or <>
1	2	Vienna	<>
4	1	Freiburg	>
3	2	Munich	>
2	1	Berlin	<>
5	2	Zermatt	<>

TOURIST–HOTEL–NORD

Hochstraße 3 D-1000 Berlin 65 ☎ (030) 46 00 30

Ruhige Parklage im betriebsamen Norden von Berlin. U-Bahn, Bus, S-Bahn und Taxi vor der Tür.

Gegenüber dem Humboldthain.
Am Bahnhof „Gesundbrunnen".
5 Autominuten vom Flughafen Tegel.

3 Study the advert above and answer the questions.

1 In welcher Straße steht das Hotel?

2 Steht das Hotel in der Stadtmitte?

3 Wie kommt man zu dem Hotel?

4 Wie heißt der nächste Bahnhof?

5 Wie kommt man in fünf Minuten zum Flughafen?

4 You are camping near your penfriend's home and he/she wants to spend a day with you. Phone him/her with instructions how to find your tent.

– You are on the Eichenwald campsite south of the town.

– Your tent is blue and it's behind the washrooms, under a big tree.

– To get there, turn left at the entrance and walk past the shop.

– You will expect him/her at about 10 o'clock.

1 Study the street map of Hamelin. Work in pairs and take turns to ask each other the way to different places, starting from the bus park. Include plenty of detail. For example, your conversation might go like this:

PUPIL 1

Entschuldigen Sie bitte, wo ist die Marktkirche?

PUPIL 2

Die steht mitten in der Stadt, in der Fußgängerzone.

PUPIL 1

Wie komme ich am besten dorthin?

PUPIL 2

Am besten gehen Sie hier über den Ostertorwall, dann die Bäckerstraße entlang bis zur Osterstraße. Die Marktkirche steht hinter dem Hochzeitshaus.

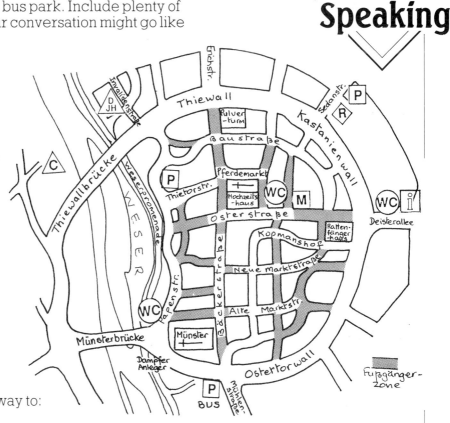

Now ask each other the way to:

a) the town hall ⟨R⟩

b) the tourist office [i]

c) the museum [M]

d) the Neue Marktstraße

e) the Weser Promenade

f) the campsite ⟨C⟩

g) the youth hostel. ⟨D JH⟩

2 You have arrived at your penfriend's home and the family is asking you about your journey. Tell them using these notes.

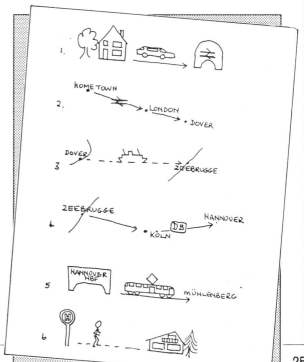

1 1 Is this ticket first or second class?

2 Is it a single or return?

3 For what form of transport was it issued?

4 What did this ticket cost?

5 For what form of transport was it used?

6 In which country was it issued?

4 1 How do you get to this car park? Does *frei* tell you there's space or that it is free of charge?

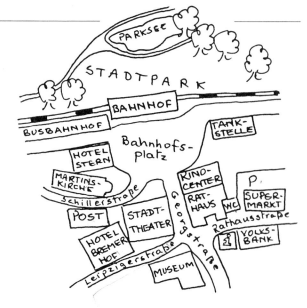

2 True or false? Study the map above.

1 Die Tankstelle ist nicht weit vom Bahnhof.

2 Es gibt keinen Park in dieser Stadt.

3 Die Post steht gegenüber der Martinskirche.

4 Das Theater ist in der Georgstraße neben dem Rathaus.

5 In der Leipzigerstraße gibt es ein Hotel.

6 Die Toiletten befinden sich zwischen dem Rathaus und dem Supermarkt.

7 Das Hotel Stern ist an der Ecke Bahnhofsplatz–Schillerstraße.

8 Hinter dem Supermarkt ist ein Parkplatz.

3 What was due to happen on the afternoon of Sunday, March 1st?

 Amtliche Publikation der Stadt Olten

Am Fasnachtssonntag, 1. März 1987, ist während Zeit von 13.00 bis ca. 16.00 Uhr die ganze Innenst für den Fahrzeugverkehr gesperrt.
Parkmöglichkeiten:

2 You have been parked here for just under two hours. What is the charge?

3 It is time to collect your car. What should you do?

Parkhaus im Zentrum
Öffnungszeiten:
täglich von 7⁰⁰-19⁰⁰

Parkpreise:
je angefangene 1. Stunde DM 1,—
je angefangene 2. Stunde DM 1,—
dann alle 30 Min. DM 0,50
max. pro Tag DM 10,—

Es gelten unsere allgemeinen Geschäftsbedingungen.

Erst zur Kasse - dann zum Wagen

5 This sign is at the end of the road where you are staying. Which way do you turn to get to

a) the town centre?

b) the hospital?

c) the swimming pool?

d) the football match?

6 Cycling in Munich's traffic is no fun, so the four of you decide to use the train to get out of the city.

1 When are cycles not allowed on the trains?

2 Should the four of you travel together, singly or in pairs?

3 What must you do with your cycle during the journey?

4 What warning are you given about escalators and lifts?

5 What may you not do on railway property?

Radl in S-Bahn und U-Bahn

Beachten Sie bitte bei der Mitnahme von Fahrrädern in den Schnellbahnen die folgenden Bestimmungen:

■ Von Montag bis Freitag dürfen Fahrräder von 6.00 bis 8.30 Uhr und von 15.00 bis 18.30 Uhr nicht mitgenommen werden.
Die Mitnahme von Fahrrädern ist an Samstagen, Sonn- und Feiertagen ganztägig erlaubt.

■ Jeder Fahrgast darf nur ein Fahrrad mitnehmen.

■ Je Einstiegsraum dürfen nur zwei Fahrräder untergebracht werden.

■ Der Fahrgast muß bei seinem Fahrrad bleiben und dieses festhalten.

Bitte beachten Sie:
Der Transport der Fahrräder ist nur über feste Treppen, nicht über Rolltreppen und in Aufzügen gestattet. Radfahren innerhalb der Schnellbahnanlagen ist verboten.

Neustadt B6 bis hinter die Brücke – auf den Parkplatz. Da ist ein großes Faß.

Auf der Seite am Faß in die Stadt gehen ca. 4–6 Häuser rechts, eine kleine Brücke + das Eckhaus nach der Brücke ist Kollmeier.

7 You were given these directions for finding Kollmeier's shop.

1 How far along the B6 towards Neustadt should you go?

2 You are told to use a large barrel (Faß) as a landmark. Where is it?

3 Whereabouts is Kollmeier's shop?

3
HIGHER
Reading

1 This advert is for a car-sharing scheme.

   1 How does the scheme help car owners?

   2 What must they do to take part?

   3 What is the advantage of this scheme if you have no car?

   4 Do you need to take out extra insurance?

2 1 Was this ticket sold individually or as part of a saver-strip?

   2 What are you told to do with it?

   3 How long is the ticket valid?

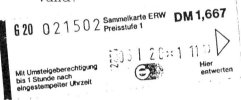

FAHR MIT – SPAR SPRIT!

43 Mitfahrzentralen im gesamten Bundesgebiet

Damit ermöglichen wir allen Autofahrern und Mitfahrern, ihre Reisekosten erheblich zu senken.

Als **Autofahrer** rufen Sie einige Tage vor Ihrer Fahrt an und stellen 1-3 freie Plätze zur Verfügung. Wir vermitteln Ihnen nette Leute – sie erhalten eine Kostenbeteiligung. Die Vermittlung der Mitfahrer ist für sie kostenlos.

Als **Mitfahrer** fragen Sie – auch kurzfristig – nach freien Plätzen. Sie fahren dabei sehr preiswert und bequem mit und sind dabei im Rahmen der Kfz-Haftpflichtversicherung des Fahrzeughalters mitversichert. Auf Wunsch können Sie bei uns gegen eine geringe Gebühr eine zusätzliche private Unfallversicherung abschließen.

Einige Preisbeispiele* für die Kostenbeteiligung von Hildesheim nach:

INLAND			AUSLAND	
Berlin	23,– DM	Kiel	23,– DM	Amsterdam	37,– DM
Bonn	31,– DM	Köln	28,– DM	Athen	175,– DM

3 Describe in detail what the holder of this ticket is entitled to.

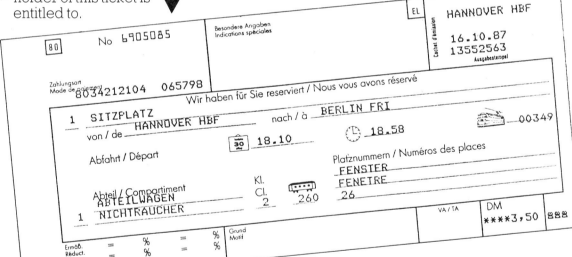

4 You are on the motorway.

   1 What is 2 kilometres ahead?

   2 What is 1.2 kilometres ahead?

   3 What is 1.6 kilometres ahead?

5
1 Which places does the EuroCity serve?

2 What should normally last for five minutes?

3 Where do customs checks take place?

4 Do EuroCity trains offer basic or more luxurious facilities?

HEISSER TIP: JETZT 'NE EUROPA-REISE!

Mit höherem Komfort reist man jetzt durch Europa - mit der Bahn

Genauer gesagt: Mit dem neuen EuroCity. Schnell, pünktlich und komfortabel wie der Intercity. Der neue EuroCity verbindet über 200 Städte in 13 Ländern Westeuropas. Mit 118 Tages- und 16 Nacht-zügen. Letztere mit Schlaf- und Liegewagen. Frühstück, Mittag- und Abendessen werden in allen EC-Zügen angeboten. Zwischendurch auch kleine Snacks und Getränke. EC-Züge sind schnelle Züge. Deshalb soll die Aufenthaltszeit auf Bahnhöfen - auch Grenzbahnhöfen - so kurz wie möglich sein und 5 Minuten im allgemeinen - bei besonderen Behandlungen 15 Minuten - nicht überschreiten. Zoll- und Grenz-kontrollen sollen grundsätzlich im Zug stattfinden. Bei Nachtreisen erledigt der Schlaf- oder Liegewagenbetreuer gern die nötigen Formalitäten für Sie. Der neue EuroCity - schon alleine ein Grund für Ihre nächste Europareise. (Frankfurt/M.)

Zeichnu

Sonntags mit dem Auto in den Urlaub

Wer mit dem Auto in die Ferien fahren möchte, sollte dies an einem Sonntag tun. Denn, so er-mittelte der ADAC, freitags und samstags sind die Auto-bahnen voll von Kurzstrecken-fahrern und Ausflüglern. Für die sichere und streßarme Au-toreise empfehlen die Verkehrs-Mediziner regelmäßige Fahr-pausen und raten, spätestens zehn Stunden nach der Abfahrt zu übernachten. Professor Willi Wirths, Bonn, rät zu fünf Mahlzeiten, die über den Rei-setag verteilt werden sollten. Sehr wichtig sei auch ausrei-chendes Trinken, am besten Tee und Mineralwasser, insge-samt 1,5 Liter pro Person.

6
1 Who is this passage aimed at?

2 Why are Sundays said to be better than Fridays and Saturdays?

3 What can be done to make long journeys safer?

4 What special advice comes from Professor Wirths?

Von Haus zu Haus – Gepäck voraus

IHRE BAHNREISE KÜNFTIG OHNE LÄSTIGES KOFFERTRAGEN!

Der Haus-Gepäckservice der 🚆 löst dieses Problem in Zusammenarbeit mit der Post

WIE GEHT DAS?

Bitte rufen Sie Ihr Postamt an und sagen: „Ich möchte mein Reisegepäck abholen lassen".

7
1 What service does this leaflet advertise?

2 Who operates the service?

3 How do you contact the service, and what should you say?

3 BASIC Writing

1 Study the letter Tim sent to Uwe after he had spent a few days at Uwe's home. Now write a similar letter to your penfriend Natascha. Your trip home wasn't so pleasant. The train arrived in Ostend on time, but the boat was very full and the weather terrible, so you did not sleep. You arrived almost an hour late in Dover. The train to London was still waiting. You were home by 9 am; you went straight to bed, you were so tired.

2 You have just spent a long weekend in Munich at the time of the beer festival. Your father won the trip in a competition. You flew there of course, and did a lot of sightseeing. You saw the zoo (Tierpark Hellabrunn), a museum, the sports facilities built for the 1972 Olympic Games (Olympiapark), and went twice to the Theresienwiese where the beer festival is held. You went to some places by underground, and others by tram or bus, and sometimes you walked.

You kept a brief diary. You wrote down where you went (in the left-hand column), how you got there (in the middle column) and what you saw or did (in the column on the right).

Manchester, den 11. April

Lieber Uwe!
Es war wirklich schön bei Dir!
Vielen Dank!
Ich bin gut nach Hause gekommen.
Der Zug ist mit fünf Minuten
Verspätung in Ostende angekommen,
sonst war alles pünktlich.
Die Überfahrt war herrlich
– ich konnte sogar drei Stunden
lang schlafen!
Meine Eltern haben mich am
Bahnhof abgeholt – bis elf Uhr
waren wir zu Hause!
Schöne Grüße, auch an
Deine Eltern,
Dein Tim.

FREITAG	nach München	mit dem Flugzeug	mein erster Flug!
– ABEND			
SAMSTAG			
–NACHMITTAG			
SONNTAG			
– ABEND			
MONTAG	nach London		

1 Your Swiss penfriend's family will be coming to visit you in a few weeks' time. You live on a new estate which does not appear on any maps. Write a letter of about 120 words to Herr Figini that includes the following points:

- Acknowledge their last letter.

- Say how much your family is looking forward to meeting them on the 14th.

- To find your house, leave the motorway (give its number) at exit 21.

- Drive straight on until third set of traffic lights.

- Turn left, then first right – he should see a small church behind some trees.

- Just beyond the church turn right. It's a narrow road and quite dangerous.

- After about 300 metres turn right again into a new road – your house is the second white one on the left.

- Say you hope they won't get lost!

- Ask what time their flight is due to arrive.

- Sign off with best wishes for a safe journey.

2 Study the pictures below, then tell the story in German in about 100 words.

4 BASIC Listening

Shopping

1 You will hear a woman buying goods in five different shops. Write down in English everything she buys. You will hear each section of the tape twice. ▶

Shop 1

Shop 2

Shop 3

Shop 4

Shop 5

2 You have been shopping at the market, and the stallholder is adding up your bill. You will hear the extract twice.

How many different things did you buy?

What was the total amount you paid?

3 You will hear a conversation between an English girl and her German penfriend's father. The tape is in sections. You will hear each section twice.

Section 1

Who does she need a present for?

What present does the man suggest she could buy?

Section 2

Which department of the Kaufhof store should she go to?

Section 3

When would she like to go?

4 Listen carefully to these five radio commercials. You will hear each one twice. Decide what each commercial is advertising. ▶

Advert 1 –

Advert 2 –

Advert 3 –

Advert 4 –

Advert 5 –

1 Listen carefully to the following five commercials from German radio. Then answer the questions below. You will hear each commercial twice.

Advert 1

The woman has just returned from Karstadt, a large department store.

1 What did she get at Karstadt?

2 Give two reasons why customers should choose Karstadt.

Advert 2

3 What kind of product is being advertised?

4 What size is the packet?

5 Give one reason for buying this size of packet.

Advert 3

6 Name the newspaper advertised here.

7 Describe one of the articles in it this week.

Advert 4

8 Which people is the advert aimed at?

9 Give two situations for which *Dextro-Energen* is recommended.

Advert 5

10 Who would this product appeal to?

11 Give two quite different things you could read about.

2 Richard is buying trousers in Germany. Listen carefully to the conversation he has with the shopkeeper, then answer the questions. The conversation is in sections. You will hear each section twice.

Section 1

1 What colour trousers does Richard want?

2 What size is Richard?

3 Is he offered a smaller or a larger pair?

Section 2

4 What is wrong with the trousers?

5 The shop has trousers in the right colour and size. Why is Richard not interested in them?

6 Why has the shop sold so many pairs of grey trousers?

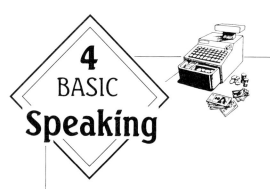

4 BASIC Speaking

1 Work in pairs. Take turns to play the customer and the shop assistant. For more practice vary the items, amounts and prices.

a) *In der Bäckerei-Konditorei*

CUSTOMER	ASSISTANT
Greet the assistant.	Greet the customer.
Ask for a white loaf.	Ask: large or small?
Say large, please.	Give the customer the loaf.
Ask how much it costs.	Tell him/her.
Write down the total in figures on a piece of paper and hand it over.	Check that the 'money' is correct. Thank him/her and say goodbye.

b) *Auf dem Markt*

CUSTOMER	ASSISTANT
Greet the stallholder, and ask for three oranges and two pounds of apples.	Hand them over. Ask if he/she wants anything else.
Ask how much the grapes cost.	Say they cost DM 2.80 a kilo.
Say you'd like a pound.	Hand them over. Ask if that is all.
Say yes. Ask what it comes to.	Say the total is DM 7.60.
Hand over a DM 10 note.	Give the customer the correct change and say goodbye.

c) *Im Schuhgeschäft*

CUSTOMER	ASSISTANT
Say you'd like a pair of sandals.	Ask what size.
Say 38 or 40.	Say you only have them in two colours. (Choose whichever colours you like.)
Ask to see the sandals in one of these colours.	Show the sandals to him/her.
Ask what they cost.	Make up a price.
Say you'll have them.	Tell the customer to pay at the cash desk.

d) *In der Weinhandlung*

CUSTOMER	ASSISTANT
Say you'd like a bottle of wine.	Ask if he/she would like German wine.
Say yes, you'd like a good wine.	Ask if he/she likes sweet wine.
Say no, not too sweet.	Ask if he/she wants red or white wine.
Choose whichever you like.	Say this wine is very good and not too expensive.
Say you'll take that bottle.	

1 Beantworten Sie:

1 Welche Kaufhäuser gibt es in Ihrer Nähe?

2 Was halten Sie von großen Einkaufszentren?

3 Wer macht bei Ihnen die Einkäufe?

4 Wo steht der nächste Supermarkt? Wie heißt er?

5 Welche Kleidungsstücke haben Sie neulich gekauft? Wo?

6 Was kaufen Sie mit Ihrem Taschengeld?

7 Wie oft kaufen Sie Schallplatten oder Musikkassetten?

8 Was würden Sie kaufen, wenn Sie ganz viel Geld hätten?

2 Work in pairs. Take it in turns to play each part.

CUSTOMER	SALES ASSISTANT
Greet the assistant and explain that you would like to exchange this jacket.	Warum eigentlich?
Say there is a button missing.	Darf ich mal sehen? Wann haben Sie die Jacke gekauft?
Say you bought it yesterday afternoon, just before 6 o'clock.	Ach ja, ich habe Sie bedient. Es tut mir leid, aber wir haben keine Jacken mehr in weiß.
Ask if you can have your money back.	Das geht leider nicht. Sie dürfen aber gerne die Jacke gegen eine andere tauschen.
Say you don't want to do that.	Es gibt aber keine andere Möglichkeit.
Exclaim that you can see the button – it's on the floor!	Wo denn? Ich sehe ihn nicht.
Say it's next to the cash desk.	Tatsächlich! Können Sie ihn selber annähen?
Answer the question.	

3 Your German penfriend has rung to thank you for a wonderful holiday. He/she asks what you have been doing. You and your mother have just been shopping – this is what you bought:

– a dark red leather skirt (special offer)

– 2 pairs of tights to go with it

– some silk underwear

– a pair of wellington boots

– a grey cotton shirt

– a T-shirt

– a stereo system

– four airbeds

– a folding table for camping.

Work in pairs. Take turns to play the English and German-speaking friends. Add as many more details as you like, for example prices, sizes, colours, who the items are for, when they will be used etc.

4 BASIC Reading

1 What are you told to do here?

Bitte bedienen Sie sich selbst

2 Frau Müller has been shopping. Study her receipt, then answer the questions.

1 What was the first item she bought?

2 How much did she pay for:
   a) fruit and vegetables
   b) cooked meats and sausages?

3 Did she buy any cheese?

4 What cost 10 pfennigs?

5 What bread did she buy?

6 What did the bill come to?

7 How much change did she get?

```
          KAUFHOF
          HANNOVER

KOPFSALAT
KAESE                           0,99 E
KAESE                           7,50 E
WURST-FLEISCHWAREN              9,03 E
SCHLAGSAHNE 30%F               25,22 E
SCHNITZELSEELACHS               0,99 E
OBST, GEMUESE                   0,99 E
RADIESCHEN                      1,61 E
TRAGETASCHE                     1,49 E
SAHNE-KAENNCHEN 12%             0,10
* SUMME *                       0,99 E
                               48,91

BAR                            50,00
RUECKGELD                       1,09

       KAUFHOF HANNOVER
      IHR FRISCHE-SPEZIALIST

0191 10015011 15. 08. 87 1158
```

3

1 You are in the Harz mountains. It is good walking country, but you need the right outfit. Where could you buy:
   a) walking maps?
   b) walking shoes?
   c) suitable clothing?

2 Which shop sells postcards?

3 Who sells films?

4 Where could you get your films processed?

5 On your first walk to Wildemann you need refreshments. List six things you could buy at Rolf Klapproth's.

6 Why might you go to Salon Peter?

4 This is part of the directory for a large store in Frankfurt.

1 How many floors are there altogether?

2 On which floor is confectionery?

3 Which departments are on the third floor?

4 Your friend needs overalls for work; in which department might he/she find them?

5 Which department might have spares for your cycle?

6 What service is available on both the first and the fifth floors?

7 Where should you go to collect the sweatshirt you lost in the store?

8 Where is the toy department?

Wo gibt es was von A bis Z?					
A		**F**		**R**	
Alles für das Bad	3.Etage	Fahrrad-Shop	Erdgeschoß	Radio/	
Alles für das Kind	2.Etage	Fernsehen	Erdgeschoß	Fernsehreparaturannahme	1.Etage
Augen-Optiker	Erdgeschoß	Fernsprecher	1. + 5.Etage	Reisebüro	Erdgeschoß
B		Fotokopien	Erdgeschoß	Restaurants	5.Etage
Babykleidung	2.Etage	Foto-Abteilung	Erdgeschoß	**S**	
Betten-Abteilung	4.Etage	Frisiersalon	1.Etage	Spielwaren	1.Etage
Bettwäsche	3.Etage	Fundbüro	1.Etage	Sportartikel	1.Etage
Berufskleidung	2.Etage	**G**		Schallplatten	Erdgeschoß
Bodenbeläge	4.Etage	Gardinen	4.Etage	Schirme	Erdgeschoß
Bücher	Erdgeschoß	Gartencenter	3.Etage	Süßwaren	Tiefgeschoß

5 The local supermarket is advertising these products.

1 What are:
   a) *Biskin*?
   b) *Blend-a-med*?
   c) *Hakle*?
   d) *Mild und fein*?

2 What is priced by the kilogramme?

3 What does milk cost?

4 What could you buy that costs DM 1.59?

5 What is *Valensina*?

6 What containers are these products sold in?

   a) *Biskin*

   b) *Jolly Pfirsiche*

   c) *Gold Extra Konfitüre*

   d) *frische Vollmilch*

Jolly Pfirsiche 1/2 Frucht od. Williams Christ Birnen **1.59**
je 850-ml-Dose

Blend-a-med Zahncreme **2.49**
100-ml-Tube

Valensina Orangensaft od. Grapefruitsaft **1.49**
je 0,7-Liter Box

Hakle Toilettenpapier **4.98**
je 8 × 250-Bl.-Pack.

Belg. Fleischtomaten **1.98**
Kl.1
1000 g

Biskin Speiseöl **2.79**
0,75-Liter-Flasche

Gold Extra Konfitüre „Bassermann" verschiedene Sorten je 450-g-Glas **1.69**

Frische Vollmilch **–.79**
1-Liter-Packung

Jacobs Kaffee „Mild und fein" 500-g-Packung **6.48**

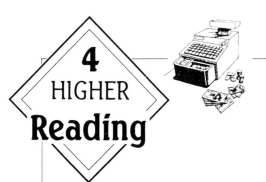

4 HIGHER Reading

1 These notices are near the entrance to a supermarket.

a) What are you asked to do?

b) What does this tell you?

c) This sign is a warning. Who is being warned?

> Bitte benutzen Sie einen
> **EINKAUFSWAGEN ODER EINEN KORB**
> damit keine Mißverständnisse entstehen

> Warenumtausch nur mit Kassenzettel

> **Den Ladendieb hat keiner Lieb**
> **Wir werden jeden Ladendieb anzeigen**

3 Explain how you could get some flowers when these shops are closed. ▼

Labor-Schnelldienst

Für ganz eilige Kunden entwickeln wir Ihren Film im eigenen Color-Labor.

Ihr Film bis 12.00 Uhr gebracht – bis 17.30 Uhr gemacht!

Ihr Film nachmittags gebracht – bis zum anderen Morgen um 9.00 Uhr gemacht!

Mit Blumen Freude schenken

Blumenparadies
Ulrich Nimz
Schillerstr. 17
Bad Pyrmont

Blumenhaus
Pietrzak
Lortzingerstr. 28
Bad Pyrmont

Nach Geschäftschluß Blumenautomaten
es werden 5 DM Stücke benötigt

4 a) What do Schmorl u. Seefeld sell?

b) Give two facts which show how large the shop is. ▼

2 This shop offers a special service.

a) What kind of shop is it?

b) Who is the special service aimed at?

c) What could you do at 9am?

Bücher in Hannover

In unserem erweiterten Hause:
Viel Platz zum Schauen und Stöbern!
Ein Superangebot in 3 Geschossen
mit über 150 000 Titeln!

...Ihre große Buchhandlung in der City

 SCHMORL ᵤᵥ SEEFELD
Bücher · Schallplatten · Landkarten
Bahnhofstraße/Große Packhofstraße

5
a) What time of year is it?

b) What kind of thing does this shop stock?

c) What does the advert imply will happen if you buy their products?

▼

Bald sind die Ferien am Ende, und die Schule geht los. Höchste Zeit, daß Sie jetzt mal in unseren Schulmarkt kommen und sich die vielen schönen Sachen für's neue Schuljahr anschauen: Bunte Füller, lustige Ringelhefte, kluge Rechner, lässige Schreibetuis, allwissende Lexika – alles, was Schüler brauchen, um in der Schule vorwärts zu kommen!

KAUFRiNG
MÜNDENER KAUFHAUS
Seit über drei Jahrzehnten mitten in Münden.

Ihr ganz persönliches Kaufhaus.

6
1 Which item for men costs DM 19?

2 What is the cheapest item?

3 What are the ties made of?

4 What costs DM 35?

5 Are the dresses more suitable for younger or older women?

6 What are we told about the shoes?

7 Are the skirts all identical, apart from their size?

▼

Damen-Nachthemden 9,-
Batist. Hübsche Modelle in ansprechenden Dessins.

Herren-Trikot-Schlafanzug 19,-
Lange Form.

Damen-Kleider 19,-
Junge und frauliche Typen, verschiedene Dessins.

Herren-Schuhe 60,-
Obermaterial Leder. Jedes Paar

Damen-Röcke 18,-
Unis oder Drucks. Verschiedene Qualitäten, Formen und Dessins. Größen 36-48.

arena Herren-Badehose 20,-
Verschiedene Formen und Farben. Größen 4-7.

Krawatten 12,-
Reine Seide

Damen-Schwimmanzug 35,-
in modischen Dessins 38-42

4 BASIC Writing

1 On holiday in Austria your family is planning a picnic. Your mother suggests you might have two rolls each, one filled with liver sausage, the other with cheese, and lots of tomatoes. All five of you would like a peach as well. Your parents decide on a bottle of beer each, you and your sisters each want a can of coke. Write yourself a shopping list in German so you will know what to ask for.

Wir brauchen :

2 Write a note of about 80 words in German to your penfriend Alexander.

- Thank him for the Christmas present.

- Say why you liked it so much.

- Say you are sending Alexander a parcel containing his birthday present.

- Say where and when you bought it.

- Say you hope he will like it.

- Wish him a happy birthday.

1 You have just had a birthday. Write a letter in German thanking your penfriend Sabine for her marvellous present. Your father gave you money to buy clothes – tell Sabine about the shopping spree you went on with your best friend. Describe what you bought, and don't forget to mention the terrific bargain you found in that big store!

2 The clock you bought in Germany last month is faulty. Write a letter of about 100 words in German to the shop where you bought it: Schwarzwaldsouvenir, Feldbergstraße 3, 7820 Titisee.

Make the following points:

- Say when you bought the clock.

- Explain that the clock goes far too fast.

- You took your clock to a repairer in your home town; she suggested a different battery, but that did not help.

- Say that you are returning the clock in a separate parcel, and that the receipt for it is attached to your letter.

- Explain that you are very disappointed with the clock. You had expected German-made goods to be of a very high quality.

- Say that you would like your money back unless the clock can be repaired quickly.

- Thank the shopkeeper in advance for his help.

Listening

Food and drink

1 You will hear several people ordering something to eat. The recording is in sections. You will hear each section twice. Listen carefully and then answer the questions below.

Section 1

1 What does the boy ask for?

2 Which flavour does he choose?

Section 2

3 What does the girl decide to have?

4 What does the boy decide to have?

Section 3

5 What kind of cake does the woman order?

6 Does she order cream?

2 You will hear a conversation between an exchange pupil and his German host family. The tape is recorded in three sections. You will hear each section of the tape twice. Copy this chart into your exercise book and complete it.

LIKES	DISLIKES	DON'T KNOW

3 You will hear four commercials from West German radio. You will hear each one twice. Listen and then answer the questions.

Advert 1

What is *La-Bamba*?

Advert 2

What kind of drink is being advertised?

Advert 3

What drink is being advertised?

Is there anything unusual about this particular brand?

Advert 4

What is *Pirshou*?

1 Two people – one a stranger to Germany – are discussing which meal to choose. Study the photograph, listen carefully to their conversation, and then decide which meal they both choose. You will hear the conversation twice.

2 It's your birthday soon after you return from Germany, and you decide to make a fruit punch (Bowle) that you had at your penfriend's home. You can't find the recipe you wrote down but you can recall a few details. You decide to phone for help. Copy into your exercise book as much of the recipe as you remember, then complete it as you listen to the tape. You will hear the recipe twice.

INGREDIENTS

Any kind of fruit?
How much?.......g
Sugar..........g
Wine (white?)
......bottles.
Anything else?

METHOD

1. Wash fruit and.....
2. Layer fruit + sugar in large bowl and add
....
3. Allow to stand for
....
4. Add...............
5. Serve............

3 You will hear three commercials from West German radio. Listen carefully, then answer the questions below. You will hear each one twice.

Advert 1

Kochlöffel is a fast-food chain.

1 What does the boy want to eat?

2 How will they order it?

3 Where will they eat it?

Advert 2

Zwieback are crispbreads.

4 Give two things which the advert suggests you eat with them.

5 Why are they suitable for weight-watchers?

Advert 3

Milchschnitte is a popular snack.

6 When does Silke need a nourishing snack?

7 List four ingredients of a *Milchschnitte*.

8 Who approves of *Milchschnitten*?

5
BASIC
Speaking

1 Work in pairs. One of you is the waiter or waitress, the other is a customer. Take turns to play each part.

CUSTOMER	WAITER
Call the waiter/waitress.	Guten Abend. Was darf es sein?
Say you'd like a fried sausage with bread, and a coke.	Ist gut. Kommt sofort. (Serve food.) So. Bitte schön.
Thank him/her, and ask for the bill.	Das macht genau fünf Mark.
Hand over the money. Say goodbye.	

WAITER	CUSTOMER
Greet the customer.	Greet the waiter and ask for the menu.
Hand it over.	Thank him.
Ask if they'd like anything to drink.	Order a beer, a glass of white wine and any kind of fruit juice you like.
Ask what they want to eat.	Say the three of you will have the roast chicken.
Offer a choice of chips or bread.	Say chips please, and salad.
Ask if they'd like soup first.	Say no thanks.
Repeat their order.	

2 Work in pairs and play each part in turn.

FRIEND 1	FRIEND 2
Ask your friend if he/she would like an ice cream.	Say yes please, you would like one costing 80 pfennigs.
Choose a different size for yourself.	Say which two flavours you would like.
Decide which flavours you're having.	Order the ice cream you've chosen.
Order the ice cream you've chosen.	Ask your friend if it tastes good.
Reply.	

1. You have spent the morning in town with your friend. It is lunchtime and you are both hungry. Work in pairs, taking turns to play each part.

FRIEND 1	FRIEND 2
Tell your friend you're terribly hungry.	Say you are, too.
Suggest you have something to eat right now.	Propose that you buy something here – the chain is called *Kochlöffel*.
Suggest what you should both have from the menu.	Disagree. Choose something different for yourself.
Ask if your friend wants salad.	Yes, you like salad. Ask what your friend wants to drink.
Suggest a drink.	Agree, you like that.
Give your order to the assistant.	Say you want it to take away, please.

2 Beantworten Sie:

1 Wo essen Sie an einem Wochentag zu Mittag?

2 Was essen Sie? Und was trinken Sie dazu?

3 Mögen Sie Kuchen und Torten? Welche Sorten?

4 Was ist Ihr Lieblingsessen?

5 Wo essen Sie gern, wenn Sie in der Stadt sind?

6 Wie oft ungefähr essen Sie in einer Gaststätte?

7 Haben Sie schon Alkohol probiert? Was? Wann? Wo?

8 Wie schmeckt Ihnen deutsches Brot oder deutsche Wurst?

9 Wer kocht bei Ihnen zu Hause?

10 Kochen Sie gern? Warum (nicht)?

3 1 Liegt dieses Restaurant in der Stadtmitte?

2 Kann man nur italienisch essen?

3 Kann man draußen sitzen? Auch bei Regen?

4 An welchem Tag ist das Restaurant geschlossen?

5 Ab wann ist das Restaurant geöffnet?

Ristorante
PINOCCHIO
Gemütliches Feinschmecker-Restaurant im Herzen der Stadt.
Wir bieten Ihnen in gemütlicher Atmosphäre italienische und internationale Spezialitäten. Im Sommer Außentische durch ein Glasdach regengeschützt. Sie finden uns in der
Andreas-Passage ca. 400 m vom Museum entfernt im 1. Obergeschoß · Telefon 0 51 21 / 3 45 45
Wir haben durchgehend geöffnet von 11.30–24.00 Uhr, kein Ruhetag.

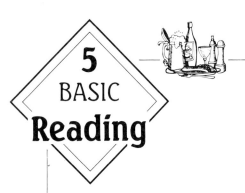

5
BASIC
Reading

1 You are looking for somewhere to have coffee and cakes. Which of these places is the one to try?

2
1 Which day is this restaurant closed?

2 Can you have lunch there on Saturdays?

3 What time does it open in the evening?

4 When is a good time to go there, according to the advert?

12–15 Uhr
18.00–1 Uhr

Vor und nach dem Theater Samstag Mittag und Sonntag geschlossen

WEINHAUS NEUNER

Münchens ältestes Weinhaus
in historischen Gewölben
Weinrestaurant · Weinstube
Telefon 2 60 39 54, Herzogspitalstraße 8, 8000 München 2

3 The Marktstube restaurant is attached to a shop.

– What kind of shop is it?
– Where is it?

4 The waiter brings this small packet with your chicken and chips. What does it contain?

a) lemon sauce   c) a damp tissue

b) fresh mayonnaise   d) salt

frisch & sauber
CITRO-TUCH

fabline

> **Reisen und Speisen hält Leib und Seele zusammen.**
> In vielen Zügen gibt es die rollenden Restaurants. Dort können Sie gut essen und trinken. Und haben nebenbei den Vorzug, daß Sie während eines guten Essens die Landschaft genießen können.
> In vielen Zügen kommt die Bar zu Ihnen, die Mini-Bar. Direkt ans Zugabteil, mit vielen belegten Broten, Bier, Kaffee, Säften und Limonaden.

5
1 Where are these restaurants? ▲
2 Where would you find the mini-bar?
3 What could you buy there?

6 At the motorway service area the menu is divided into these sections: Which section should you look at if you want: ▶

a) cakes? d) soft drinks?

b) soup? e) children's portions?

c) sausage?

> Hausgemachte Suppen
> Belegte Brote
> Aus unserer Wurstküche
> Für unsere kleinen Gäste
> Grill- und Pfannengerichte
> Kuchen
> Schwäbische Spezialitäten
> Seniorenteller
> Warme Getränke
> Erfrischungsgetränke

◀ **7** Your penfriend's parents are taking you to a new restaurant where the food is cooked in a special way.

1 Give three types of food mentioned in the advert.

2 Who does the cooking?

3 How is the food cooked?

4 What do they say about food cooked in this way?

8
1 How many kinds of ▶ cake are there?

2 How much do you pay for cream?

3 Which two things are served with ice cream?

4 What costs DM 2.50?

Neu im KomödiantenStadl:

Essen vom heißen Stein...

...ein wahrhaft "heißer" Tip für alle

Auf einem 300° heißen Naturstein aus einem geheimen Steinbruch in den Alpen grillen Sie selbst: Fleisch, Fisch, Gemüse, Brot. Das schafft Atmosphäre, macht Spaß und schmeckt einmalig gut!

KomödiantenStadl
Bräuhausstraße 8 · 8000 München 2 · Tel. 089/29 74 03
Täglich ab 19 Uhr bis 3 Uhr früh.

KUCHEN UND EIS-SPEZIALITÄTEN

Apfelkuchen	2,70
Käsekuchen	2,70
Himbeertorte	2,70
Portion Sahne	1,10
Gemischtes Eis	2,50
Vanilleeis mit Kirschen	3,50
Vanilleeis mit Schokoladensauce	3,50
Eiskaffee mit Schlagsahne	2,75

1 Someone has given you a packet of Pumpernickel to try.

– What kind of food is it?

– What could you eat with it?

– Where did it spend 24 hours?

2 You enjoyed dumplings (Knödel) in Germany, so your hostess gave you a pack of ready-to-cook dumplings to take home. Now you want to know what to do with them. They are individually wrapped in a cloth bag (Kochbeutel) and packed in a plastic bag (Klarsichtbeutel).

▼

1 You only want to cook three dumplings.

   a) How should you store the others?

   b) How long will they keep?

2 What should you put the dumplings into?

3 What must you be careful to do?

4 The total cooking time is 16 minutes.

   a) What should you do for 1 minute?

   b) What should you do for 15 minutes?

5 What should you do with them when they are cooked?

6 What is the last thing to do before you serve them?

3
1 Could you eat lunch here?

2 What do they serve in the afternoon?

3 Do they close at 6pm?

4 Who does the cooking?

5 What does the advert say are the advantages of eating here?

6
Kartoffel-Knödel halb und halb in Kochbeuteln

● Ungekochte Knödel sind im wieder gut verschlossenen Klarsichtbeutel mindestens 8 Wochen haltbar.

So einfach wird's gemacht:

1. Klarsichtbeutel öffnen. Gewünschte Anzahl Knödel herausnehmen.

2. Knödel in einen Topf mit kaltem, gesalzenem Wasser legen. Sie müssen gut mit Wasser bedeckt sein. Zum Kochen bringen, ca. 1 Minute kochen und 15 Minuten bei schwacher Hitze im geöffneten Topf ziehen lassen.

3. Knödel herausnehmen und kurz mit kaltem Wasser abschrecken.

4. An einem Ende des Kochbeutels aufreißen. Knödel heiß servieren.

5 HIGHER
Reading

4 Read the passage on the right, then answer the questions.

1 What do children need in the morning, according to the experts?

2 What still happens, despite the experts' advice?

3 Why should children not be forced to eat a big breakfast?

4 What is suggested as the basis of a good breakfast?

5 What four things could be served in addition?

Nicht umsonst haben Ärzte und Ernährungsexperten immer wieder darauf hingewiesen, wie falsch es ist, ein Kind ohne ausreichendes Frühstück in die Schule gehen zu lassen. Trotzdem gibt es noch immer Kinder, die ohne etwas gegessen und getrunken zu haben zum Unterricht kommen.

Es muß kein füllendes, erzwungenes Frühstück sein, denn es gibt Kinder, die morgens schwer aufwachen und nichts essen wollen, weil „der Magen noch schläft". Aber ein Frühstück muß sein! Ein warmes Getränk, frische Brötchen oder Brot vom Bäcker, Haferflocken und, von Kindern am liebsten angenommen, frisches Gebäck. Dazu individuell verschieden Butter, Honig, Marmelade oder eine Scheibe Wurst, ganz was dem Junior am besten schmeckt.

5 This is part of a brochure from the town of Celle where you are on holiday. Study the adverts before answering the questions.

1 Does the City–Bacchus–Grill open only at lunchtime?

2 Could you have lunch at the Allerkrug next Sunday?

3 It's Saturday evening. Can you eat at Gasthaus Stute?

4 Where exactly is Kraemer's café?

5 Which place sells take-away food?

6 Which is the best place to try a local speciality?

7 What time does Kraemer's café close on Saturdays?

Cafés / Konditoreien
Bier- und Weinlokale · Tanzbars
Restaurants · Spezialitäten-Restaurants

*Kraemer, Stechbahn 7, gegenüber der Stadtkirche, Tel. 21 74 21. Tagescafé, 150 Plätze. Geöffnet täglich von 7.00 bis 18.30 Uhr, sonnabends 7.00 bis 14.00 Uhr, geschäftsoffener Sonnabend 7.00 bis 18.00 Uhr, sonntags von 14.00 bis 18.00 Uhr.

Bürgerstube, Bergstraße 34, Tel. 2 37 19. Speiserestaurant. Geöffnet (außer dienstags) von 11.00 bis 23.00 Uhr, sonntags 10.00 bis 23.00 Uhr, durchgehend warme Küche.

Dalmatia-Grill, Kanzleistraße 6, Tel. 68 91 · Balkan- und internationale Spezialitäten vom Holzkohlengrill, 100 Plätze · Geöffnet von 12.00 bis 15.00 Uhr und 17.45 bis 24.00 Uhr.

City-Bacchus-Grill-Restaurant, Leckerbissen aus der griechischen Küche. Im Zentrum von Celle. Täglich von 11.00 bis 1.00 Uhr. Innenstadt. Durchgehend warme Küche. Aus-dem-Fenster-Verkauf für den kleinen Hunger.

Gasthaus Stute, Restaurant, Hannoversche Straße 42, Tel. 2 59 93. Speisegaststätte mit Celler Spezialitäten. Sonntags bis freitags ab 18.00 Uhr geöffnet. Sonnabends Ruhetag.

Allerkrug, Gaststätte und Speiselokal, Alte Dorfstraße 14, 3100 Celle, Ortsteil Altencelle, Tel. 8 48 94. Täglich geöffnet von 11.30 bis 14.30 Uhr und 18.00 bis 2.00 Uhr, Küche von 11.30 bis 14.30 Uhr und von 18.00 bis 23.00 Uhr. Dienstags Ruhetag. Großer Parkplatz vorhanden.

49

5 BASIC
Writing

Frühstück ....
Mittagessen ....
Kaffee und Kuchen .....
Abendbrot ....

1 Yesterday was your first full day in Germany and your first experience of German food. Your hosts told you the German name for everything you ate. How much can you remember?

2 Study this passage, then answer the questions in German.

1 Was trinken Dirk und Ole?

2 Was muß Britta jeden Tag mitnehmen?

3 Wieviele Schüler nehmen Brot mit?

4 Was für Obst essen diese Schüler?

5 Wer nimmt Schokolade mit?

6 Was ißt du in der Pause?

7 Was trinkst du am liebsten, oder trinkst du gar nichts?

8 Was schmeckt dir am besten – Butterbrote, Kartoffelchips oder Schokolade?

9 Welche Obstsorten ißt du gern?

10 Wer in deiner Klasse bringt Butterbrote für die Pause mit?

Geschmacksache(n)
Was Schüler in der Pause essen.

DIRK (13): „Ich esse in der Pause am liebsten ein **Wurstbrot**. Meine Mutter gibt mir auch immer **Obst** mit. Entweder eine **Apfelsine** oder eine **Banane**. Und dann habe ich auch noch was **Süßes** dabei! Und zu trinken habe ich gerne eine **Tüte Milch**."

OLE (13): „Ein paar **Schnitten Brot** müssen schon sein! Ich trinke dazu meistens einen **Saft, Orangensaft** oder so. Oder ich nehme mir von zuhause eine **Banane** mit. Naja, und natürlich was **Süßes**, zum Beispiel **Lakritz** oder einen Schokoladenriegel."

BRITTA (16): „Zur Schule nehm' ich eine **Scheibe Brot** und einen **Apfel** mit. Also, der Apfel muß immer sein. Ich komme gar nicht auf die Idee, eine Tafel Schokolade oder sowas mitzunehmen. Einige Leute aus meiner Klasse  fangen schon in der ersten Pause mit einer Tüte Kartoffelchips an!"

1 Write a letter of about 120 words in German to your penfriend. Make the following points:

- Thank the family for suggesting you could put your caravan in their garden for three nights. You will be arriving on the 24th July.

- It is your mother's birthday whilst you are there, and your father wants to take everyone out for a meal.

- Can they recommend somewhere nice with plenty of choice, not too expensive?

- You'd like typical German food, perhaps local specialities.

- Ask them to book a table for eight for the 25th July.

- Ask them not to mention it in their next letter – the meal is to be a surprise for your mother.

2 Your penfriend so enjoyed your mother's Yorkshire pudding that he took home the recipe for his family, but you have had a letter to say that their first attempt was a failure. Your mother suggests that you send him this advice, in German:

- You should make the batter (der Teig) 2 or 3 hours in advance.

- You must beat it very well.

- You should let it stand, then beat it again before you cook it.

- The oven must be very hot before you begin to cook.

- The dish and the fat or oil must also be very hot.

- You must eat Yorkshire pudding as soon as it is cooked.

3 Study the pictures below, then tell the story in German.

6 BASIC Listening

1 You will hear a tourist attempting to find accommodation. Listen carefully and then answer the questions. You will hear each section of the tape twice.

Section 1

What rooms are available at this hotel?

Section 2

What type of room does the tourist ask for?

Section 3

What accommodation does the receptionist offer?

Section 4

How much does the room cost?

What does the tourist ask to do?

Section 5

Does she decide to accept the room?

2 You will hear a boy booking in at a youth hostel. You will hear each section twice. Listen and then answer the questions.

Section 1

1 How long does he want to stay?

2 What does the warden ask to see?

Section 2

3 Where is the boy's bed?

4 Has he brought his own sleeping bag?

5 When is the evening meal?

3 You have phoned a German campsite to ask for information. Copy the chart below into your exercise book, then listen carefully to the tape and fill in the information you are given. The tape is in three sections. You will hear each section twice.

Charges for
Caravan   ...Marks
adults   ...
children   ...
Car   ...
hot showers   ...
Any other facilities?
How busy in July?
Can we book?
How?

4 You will hear a weather report from West German television. The tape is in sections. You will hear each section twice.

Section 1

What was today's weather like in southern Germany?

Section 2

What is tomorrow's forecast for northern districts?

Section 3

What will the weather be like tomorrow in the south-west?

1 You will hear a group of young people chatting about their holidays. Listen carefully and answer the questions below. You will hear each section of the tape twice.

Section 1

1. What two things did the boy travel to England for?

2. Where did the girl go?

3. Who did she travel with?

4. Describe her reaction to the trip.

Section 2

5. Where did the boy spend his holiday?

6. What did he do there?

7. Explain what the girl felt about her holiday.

8. What has she got to look forward to?

2 You are listening to the early morning weather report on the radio. You are hoping the weather will be fit for a trip up the Zugspitze, Germany's highest mountain. What was the weather like on the Zugspitze at 6.30am? You will hear the extract twice.

3 You will hear a family discussing their plans for the afternoon. Listen carefully to the tape, then answer the questions. You will hear the discussion twice.

1. What do three members of the family want to do?

2. Explain why it seems such a good idea.

3. Why did the mother suggest something else?

4. What treat can she expect for giving in so easily?

4 Frau Seeli is giving an interview about her home town of Interlaken. The tape is in sections. You will hear each section twice.

Section 1

1. What does Frau Seeli like about living in Interlaken?

2. Why does she think herself luckier than the holidaymakers?

Section 2

3. What does Frau Seeli feel about the presence of so many tourists in Interlaken?

4. Why are tourists important for Frau Seeli and her husband?

5. How long is the tourist season in Interlaken?

6 BASIC
Speaking

1 It is your first day in Germany. You're in the Verkehrsamt asking for information. Work in pairs, taking turns to play each part.

TOURIST	ASSISTANT
Ask what there is to see in the town.	Say a church, a museum, a castle.
Ask when the museum is open.	Every day from 10am to 4.30pm.
Ask if you can visit the castle.	Only on Sundays.
Ask where you can get tickets for the folk evening (Heimatabend).	Here in the tourist office.
Ask if there is an open-air swimming pool in the area.	Say yes, near the castle.
Ask what time the bank closes.	At 6pm today.
Ask if tomorrow's weather will be good.	No, it will be cool and wet.
Ask if they have a street map.	Yes, and it is free of charge.

2 Your family needs overnight accommodation. You have found a pleasant-looking Gasthaus. Work in pairs, taking turns to play each part.

GUEST	RECEPTIONIST
Ask if they have a double room with bath and toilet, and a single room.	Ask how long they are staying.
Say just one night.	Say you have two doubles but no singles.
Ask what the rooms cost.	Say double rooms cost DM 60.
Check the price includes breakfast.	Say yes, breakfast is included.
Ask to see the rooms.	Say yes and ask them to come with you.

3 Work in pairs. Take turns to play the part of the campsite warden and the tourist on holiday with a friend.

WARDEN	TOURIST
Guten Abend.	Greet the warden. Ask if there's space for a tent.
Platz haben wir hier am Eingang, oder drüben neben den Waschräumen.	Make your choice.
Wie alt seid ihr?	Tell him/her both your ages.
Ihr seid also keine Kinder mehr. Die Gebühr beträgt 3 Mark pro Person.	Ask what the tent costs.
Noch zwei Mark dazu.	Ask if they have hot showers.
Ja. Warmwasser ist inklusive. Also, ich bekomme von euch acht Mark.	Hand it over.

1 Using this diary, describe what you did each day of your holiday. Add further details if you wish.

13 Wednesday	Arrived in Füssen – hotel beautiful – rooms large and clean – lovely view over town
14 Thursday	morning: wandered around Füssen afternoon: up Tegelberg by cable car. Sunny all day.
15 Friday	Bus trip to Munich – huge city, very interesting – saw several churches and a big museum – must go back.
16 Saturday	Morning: shopping Afternoon: bus trip into Austria – magnificent scenery
17 Sunday	The hottest day yet, swimming in lake, barbecued fish for lunch. Violent thunderstorm during night.
18 Monday	Cool and misty.. visited Schloss Neuschwanstein with hundreds of American tourists
19 Tuesday	Weather nice again, didn't do much except swim and sunbathe.

2 Work in pairs. Take it in turns to ask and answer these questions.

1 Wenn Sie in Urlaub fahren, übernachten Sie meistens auf einem Campingplatz, in einem Hotel, oder woanders? Was ist schöner?

2 Haben sie ein Zelt oder einen Wohnwagen? Beschreiben Sie es/ihn.

3 Warum übernachten so viele junge Leute in Jugendherbergen, glauben Sie?

4 Waren Sie schon im Ausland? Wo waren Sie? Wie lange haben Sie dort verbracht? Wie hat es Ihnen dort gefallen?

5 Wo haben Sie letzten Sommer Urlaub gemacht? Wie sind Sie dorthin gekommen?

6 Was ist schöner, finden Sie, Urlaub an der Küste oder in den Bergen? Warum?

7 Erklären Sie, warum Sie (nicht) gern in die Schweiz oder nach Deutschland fahren möchten.

8 Warum verbringen so viele Briten ihren Urlaub in südlichen Ländern?

9 Wenn Sie Winterurlaub machen würden, würden Sie Schnee oder Sonne suchen? Warum?

10 Wohin fahren Sie nächsten Sommer?

3 Study the pictures below, then tell the story in German.

Ihr nächster Tag Urlaub. Ein Ausflug auf Rhein und Mosel – mit Bahn und Schiff.
Die Weiße Flotte der KD-Ausflugsschiffe fährt täglich auf Rhein und Mosel, vorbei an den schönsten Landschaften. Von April bis Oktober. Mit der Bahn sind Sie schnell an einer der vielen Anlegestellen der KD. Alles Nähere am Fahrkartenschalter.

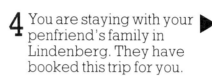

KD Köln-Düsseldorfer [DB] **Deutsche Bundesbahn**

1 Why would there be no point in asking here for a room?

GÄSTEZIMMER

BESETZT   BESETZT

2 At the entrance to the campsite you find this notice.

Anmeldung
bitte
im Wohnhaus
200 Meter links

– Where does it tell you to go?

– Why must you go there?

3 1 What sort of trip is advertised here?

2 When do the trips run?

3 Where can you get further information?

4 You are staying with your penfriend's family in Lindenberg. They have booked this trip for you.

1 When precisely will you be going?

2 What will happen when you get to Meersburg?

Termin
Di. 15. 04.

Ziel

Kaffeefahrt nach Meersburg, von dort machen wir einen Spaziergang auf dem Uferweg nach Hagnau, ca. 3 km, mit dem Bus zurück nach Lindenberg

Abfahrt 13.00
DM **12,—**

5 Your family would like to book a bus tour for next Saturday.

1 Explain to your parents where the first trip will take you.

2 What sort of place is Mainau?

3 What extra cost will there be on the first trip?

4 What sort of sights are included on the second

SAMSTAG

8.55 **Dreiländerfahrt-
"Rund um den Bodensee"**
Deutsche Alpenstraße-
Lindau-Meersburg-Tropeninsel
Mainau-Konstanz-
St. Margrethen-Bregenz.
DM 23,- + Fähre

10.25 **Wieskirche-
Königsschlösser-Füssen**
Besuch der berühmtesten
Rokokokirche Deutschlands;
Schloß Neuschwanstein und
Hohenschwangau. DM 23,-

6 Your parents suggest you might like to go to the Munich zoo at Hellabrunn. What is the special attraction at the moment?

Komm zu uns nach Hellabrunn

Viele Jungtiere jetzt zu sehen

7 List three things that you could see in this museum. ▼

Besuchen Sie das liebenswerteste Museum in Goslar das sehr bekannte

Puppen-Museum

mit der entzückenden Puppen-und Spielzeugsammlung

im

Musikinstrumente-Museum Goslar

Hoher Weg 5
(zwischen Markt u. Kaiserpfalz)

Wir zeigen 5 Ausstellungen für 1x Eintritt

Täglich geöffnet 10-18 Uhr

9 Your parents are looking at holiday possibilities.

1 What kind of holiday is this?

2 When would you take this holiday?

3 Give two advantages of going at this particular time.

Vorweihnachtsski

Freuen Sie sich auf den ersten Schnee. In den hochgelegenen alpinen Skigebieten beginnt die Saison schon im November. Die Pisten gehören Ihnen, keine langen Wartezeiten an den Liften, und das zu günstigen Preisen.

4 What kind of holiday is ▼ this?

5 Who is it aimed at?

Ferien für Kinder.
Jede Menge Platz,
auf dem Hof, auf dem Feld.
Und Tiere zum Anfassen.
Ferien.
Auf einem Bauernhof.
In Bayern.

8 You are on holiday in Hof, Bavaria, ▶ and the weather has been awful.

1 What was unusual about this frost?

2 When did it happen?

3 What 'honour' did Hof have?

Frost im Sommer

HOF (ddp) Bodentemperaturen von minus ein Grad und Lufttemperaturen um ein Grad plus ließen die Menschen in der Nacht von Donnerstag auf Freitag in Hof erschauern.

Im Hochsommermonat August war das oberfränkische Hof damit nach Angaben des Deutschen Wetterdienstes einen Tag lang die „kälteste Stadt Deutschlands".

1
1 What kind of place is this?
2 What three services does it offer?

FREMDENVERKEHRSAMT MÜNCHEN
Postanschrift: Postfach, 8000 München 1
Telex: 524801 fras d
Touristische Auskünfte: Sammel-Nr. (089) 23911
Auskunft, Prospekte, Zimmervermittlung

CAMPING-SPASS

Für Campingreisen in die DDR erhalten Sie einen Gutschein, der bei Einreise in die DDR an den unten genannten Grenzübergangsstellen in Mark der DDR eingetauscht wird.

● Die Einreise kann nur über folgende Straßenübergangsstellen erfolgen: Hirschberg, Wartha, Marienborn, Horst, Zarrentin, Selmsdorf, Warnemünde, Saßnitz, Zinnwald, Görlitz und Worbis. An den genannten Grenzübergangsstellen wird der von uns ausgestellte Gutschein in Mark der DDR eingetauscht. Hiervon werden dann die Campingplatzgebühren bezahlt. Diese betragen pro Person und Übernachtung 4 bis 10 Mark je nach Saison und Standort. Kinder von 6–14 Jahren erhalten 50 % Ermäßigung auf die Übernachtungsgebühr.

● Die zusätzliche Stellplatzgebühr für Zelte beträgt 6 Mark, für Caravans und Wohnmobile 10 Mark.

Kostenlose
Wander- und Bergwanderführungen des Kur- und Fremdenverkehrsamtes

Treffpunkt: Dienstag um 9.00 Uhr am »Haus des Gastes«.

Sollte am Dienstag die jeweils ausgeschriebene Tour wegen schlechtem Wetter nicht durchgeführt werden können, so wird diese bei entsprechender Witterung am Donnerstag nachgeholt. Treffpunkt und Uhrzeit wie Dienstag!
Bitte beachten: Gutes Schuhwerk ist erforderlich. Die Mitnahme von Regenbekleidung und einer kleinen Brotzeit im Rucksack ist empfehlenswert.

Wanderung zum Schönkahler, 1687 m

Mit dem Bus ab dem »Haus des Gastes« ins Achtal. Von hier Aufstieg zum Schönkahler (1687 m). Abstieg übers »Ächsele« zur Bärenmoosalp und von hier ins Achtal und zurück zum »Haus des Gastes«.   Gehzeit: ca. 6 Stunden

Engetal – Breitenberg, 1838 m

Mit dem Bus ab dem »Haus des Gastes« ins Achtal bis zum Zollamt Enge (Ausweise nicht vergessen!). Von hier Aufstieg über die Jägerhütte zur Ostlerhütte (1838 m), von hier Abstieg zur Fallmühle und zurück zum »Haus des Gastes«.   Gehzeit: ca. 6 Stunden

2 Your neighbours have been enquiring about camping in East Germany next summer. They were sent this information. When they book the holiday, they will be sent a voucher (Gutschein).

1 What will happen to this voucher?
2 What is the charge for an adult?
3 What is the charge for a child?
4 What is the charge for a tent?

3 These expeditions are led by qualified mountain guides.

1 When do they normally take place?
2 What might cause a walk to be postponed?
3 What advice is given about equipment etc?
4 How long is the walk to the Schönkahler?
5 What extra item do you need on the Breitenberg walk?
6 What does it cost to take part?

Wärmster Tag des Jahres mit 28 Grad: Der Sommer ist da!

Am Samstag, dem bisher wärmsten Tag des Jahres, wurden in der Rheinebene und in Teilen Süddeutschlands 28 Grad gemessen. Gestern war es nicht ganz so heiß, weil die Sonne durch die starke Bewölkung nicht durchkam. „Von Montag an wird das wieder anders, nämlich sonnig und sehr heiß bis über 30 Grad", versprach am Sonntag der Deutsche Wetterdienst.

4
1 What happened on Saturday?
2 How and why was Sunday different?
3 What will Monday be like?

5 Your aunt and uncle received this card from some old friends.

1 What did this holiday mean to Ulf and Helga?

2 How do they feel at this point in their holiday?

3 What have they found a little disappointing?

6 1 What is the main advantage of youth hostels?

2 What happened at Burg Altena?

3 List eight pastimes or hobbies that are catered for.

4 What costs DM 10?

5 How long is it valid?

6 What are you recommended to do before you set off?

▼

Cairns 23. 1. 87

Liebe Margaret, lieber Harold,
hier auf haben wir ja viele Jahre
gewartet und bald ist die Reise
schon zu Ende. Nach einem kurzen
Besuch in Indien fahren wir seit
4 Wochen durch Queensland.
Leider kann man hier im Mai
nicht baden, weil es eine giftige
Fischart gibt (Marine Stingers).
Doch morgen wollen wir noch
mal aufs Reef. Uns geht es gut!
Ganz viele Grüße Eure Ulf + Helga

Mr + M...
14 Hal...
Cawn...

7 1 Which town does this tour go to?

2 What else will you see on this tour?

3 How long is the tour that includes the 'Neue Palais'?

4 What arrangements have been made for lunch?

5 As a foreigner, what do you need to have with you on the trip?

FERIEN IN DER JUGENDHERBERGE

uxushotels sind sie nicht – unsere Jugendherbergen. Aber wer etwas erleben will, kann hier tolle Ferien zu günstigen Preisen verbringen. Erfunden wurden die Jugendherbergen von einem Lehrer: Richard Schirrmann richtete 1912 in der Burg Altena die erste Jugendherberge der Welt ein. Mittlerweile gibt es allein in der Bundesrepublik 564 Herbergen, ingesamt 54 Länder sind Mitglied im Internationalen Jugendherbergsverband.
Jugendherbergen haben ein umfangreiches Freizeitangebot: Gebirgswanderungen, Ausflüge mit dem Rad, dem Boot oder zu Pferd. Auch Kurse im Surfen, Drachenfliegen, Tennis oder Fallschirmspringen werden angeboten. Die Hobbys kommen nicht zu kurz: Töpfern, Zeichnen, Puppenbau, Pantomime, Foto- und Filmkurse sind nur einige Beispiele.
Für Jugendherbergen brauchst du einen Mitgliedsausweis. Bis 24 Jahre gilt der Juniorenausweis zu 10 DM. Damit kann man 13 Monate lang alle Jugendherbergen der Welt besuchen. Für den Antrag brauchst du eine schriftliche Einwilligung deiner Eltern.
Vor Fahrtbeginn solltest du dich am besten schriftlich anmelden, vor allem wenn die Reise länger dauert.

Potsdam — Sanssouci

in unvergeßlicher Ausflug in die Geschichte — ein Ausflug nach Potsdam: Bei dieser Tour bieten wir Ihnen eine Stadtrundfahrt durch Potsdam, die Besichtigung des Schlosses Sanssouci, der Sommerresidenz Friedrichs des Großen sowie des Parks von Sanssouci.
Die Ganztagesfahrt ist noch ausführlicher und zusätzlich wird das „Neue Palais" besichtigt.
Ein Mittagessen ist bei beiden Fahrten eingeschlossen. Voranmeldung ist erforderlich. Bundesbürger benötigen neben dem Reisepaß ein Visum. Anträge senden wir Ihnen gerne zu. Der Visaantrag in zweifacher Ausfertigung muß 30 Tage vor Fahrtantritt bei uns vorliegen.
Visagebühren für Bundesbürger DM 5,-.
Ausländer benötigen einen gültigen Reisepaß.

6 BASIC Writing

1 Your penfriend has been asking about your area. There isn't an official brochure so you decide to make up one in German. Include information about places that are worth visiting, anything interesting there is to do, the scenery, where the town or village is situated in relation to other towns, the activities and sports which are available and so on.

2 You have just spent a lovely holiday staying with your penfriend Joachim. Write a postcard in German thanking him and his mother and inviting him to your home next year. Suggest alternative dates at Easter and in the summer. On the right-hand side write an address for Joachim.

3 Your parents are planning a holiday in Switzerland. Write a letter of about 80 words in German to the Hotel Spiez in Thun booking one double and two single rooms, all with showers and toilets, from 26th July to 2nd August. Say you'd like to pay no more than 40 francs per person per night, including breakfast. Ask if the hotel also serves evening meals.

1 Write a letter of 100–120 words in German to your penfriend describing what happened on your summer holiday, real or imaginary. Explain where you went, what you did, and what the weather was like; add further details of your own.

2 Your penfriend's family is coming over for a family celebration this summer, but you won't be able to accommodate them all. Write a letter of about 100 words in German, explaining the problem. Include the following points:

– Suggest two different hotels they might like to stay at.

– Say how close they are to your home.

– Give details of accommodation, price, availability of meals etc.

3 Study the pictures below and tell the story in German. If you like, you can imagine that you were one of the group.

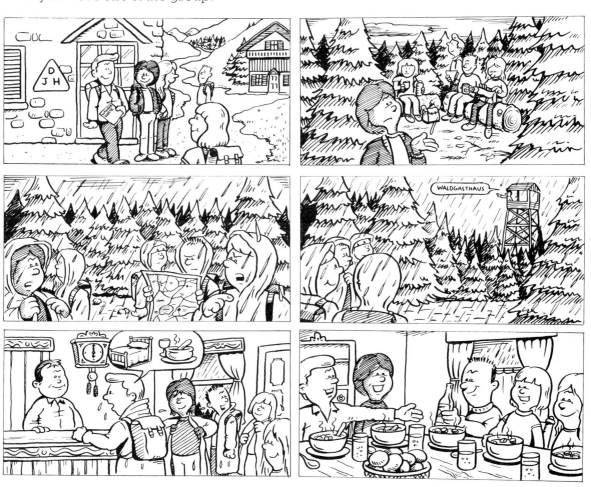

Leisure and entertainment

7 BASIC Listening

1 You will hear four short conversations in German. You will hear each of them twice. Read each question before the tape starts.

Section 1

Where are these two friends likely to spend the evening?

Section 2

What event is the boy inviting his friend to?

Section 3

What might the girl be doing at the weekend?

Section 4

Why can't the boy go swimming?

2 Your exchange partner has taken you to see a popular operetta. During the interval there is an announcement. What does it say about the second act? You will hear the announcement twice.

3 Your penfriend is busy. He has asked you to listen out for the winning numbers in the weekly Lotto competition, the result of Game 77 and two sports results. You will hear each section of the tape twice.

Section 1

1 This is your friend's entry for Lotto. List the numbers that he got right.

2 Your friend's number for Game 77 is 0407949. Did it win?

Section 2

3 Did the Stuttgarter Kickers win, lose or draw?

4 How many goals did they score?

Section 3

5 How far has Eva Pfaff got in the tennis tournament in Hamburg?

6 How many sets did she play to defeat Barbara Gerken?

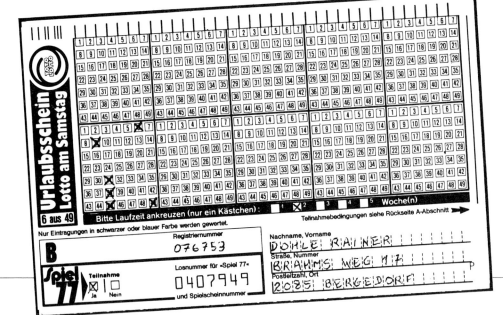

1 You will hear a boy from southern Germany being interviewed about his leisure activities. The tape is in sections. You will hear each section twice.

Section 1

1 Where does the boy live?

2 What is life like there?

Section 2

3 How many evenings does he go out?

4 Why does he attend the sports club so regularly?

Section 3

5 Which two activities does he do at weekends?

6 Who goes with him?

2 You will hear two commercials from West German radio.

Advert 1

This is for Madonna's latest album, but it also contains a piece of news. You will hear the item twice.

– What is happening?

– When?

– In which town?

Advert 2

This is for a magazine *Journal für die Frau*. You will hear it twice.

– What is the main feature in this issue?

3 You switch on the television set in your hotel room just in time to catch a preview of the evening's programmes. Answer the questions below. The tape is in three sections. You will hear each section twice.

Section 1

1 What programme begins at 8 o'clock?

2 The next programme marks a special anniversary; what is the date?

Section 2

3 They are showing a serial at 9.45; which episode is being shown tonight?

4 What topic will be discussed on the sports programme?

Section 3

5 What is the late evening film about?

6 When (approximately) will the film end?

7
BASIC
Speaking

1 Work in pairs, taking turns to play each part. One of you plays an English-speaking pupil asking about the interests of his/her German penfriend. Add some of your own questions if you like.

1 Hast du viel Freizeit?

2 Was machst du am Wochenende?

3 Gehst du gern ins Kino?

4 Welchen Sport treibst du?

5 Was siehst du am liebsten im Fernsehen?

6 Was für Musik hörst du gern?

7 Bist du in einem Verein?

8 Wieviel Taschengeld bekommst du?

2 Book two tickets for the theatre. Work in pairs. Take turns to play each part.

ASSISTANT	YOU
Guten Tag.	Ask for two tickets for *Romeo and Juliet*.
Für den wievielten?	Tell him/her.
Ich habe noch Karten im Parkett und im zweiten Rang.	Ask what they cost.
Im Parkett kostet eine Karte DM 66, im zweiten Rang DM 44.	Say which you want.
In der vierten Reihe oder in der sechsten?	Make your choice.
So. Bitte schön. Das macht DM 88.	Hand over 100 marks.
Und zwölf Mark zurück. Ich danke Ihnen.	

Staatstheater Stuttgart

```
G R O S S E S    H A U S

"ROMEO UND JULIA"                    *142

07.03.87  20:00              173

II.RANG MITTE                        ( 24 )

Reihe   4   Platz   73    DM   44,00

0101000017324004007301
```
Umtausch oder Rücknahme nicht möglich, ausgenommen bei Ausfall oder Änderung der Vorstellung. Karte bitte bis Vorstellungsschluß aufbewahren. Kein Einlaß nach Vorstellungsbeginn.

3 Study the picture below, then answer the questions.

a) Wer tanzt?

b) Was macht das Mädchen, das am Fluß liegt?

c) Was kann man draußen machen?

d) Was macht der Junge rechts vorne?

e) Was hat er in der Hand?

f) Welche Sportarten kann man in der großen Halle machen?

g) Wieviele Leute stehen vor dem Fernseher?

h) Was machen die beiden Jungen links vor dem Haus?

i) Womit spielt der Junge, der direkt in der Mitte steht?

1 Study the cutting carefully, then answer the questions.

a) Wie groß ist die Band?

b) Welchen Preis hat die Band gewonnen?

c) Was für Musik macht die Band?

d) In welcher Sprache singen sie?

e) Was macht Hartmut Engler?

f) Ist ihre Musik sehr extrem?

PUR

Pur ist eine neue fünfköpfige junge Band aus Baden-Württemberg, die Gewinner des deutschen Rockpreises 1986. Die fünf machen deutschspra-chige Rockmusik. Die Schreiber der Formation sind der Leadsänger Hart-mut Engler und der Keyboardspieler Ingo Reidl. Pur macht nette, gefällige Lieder mit eingängigen Refrains. Ihr Rock ist nicht zu rockig, eher schon bei Pop einzuordnen. Von den fünfen könnte noch einiges kommen.

2 Work in pairs. Take it in turns to play each part.

BRITISH TEENAGER	GERMAN TEENAGER
Ask what his/her favourite TV programme is.	Say *Schwarzwaldklinik* at the moment.
Say that has been on TV here. Ask if it is popular in Germany.	Say it's one of the most popular programmes. Ask if he/she saw it.
Say only once or twice.	Ask if he/she liked it.
Say not much – the scenery was pretty but you found it boring.	Say you disagree. You think young Dr Brinkmann is incredibly good-looking.
Say you found him stupid – you couldn't stand him at all!	

3 Work in pairs. Take it in turns to ask and answer these questions:

1 Welche Hobbys haben Sie?

2 Spielen Sie ein Instrument? Welches?

3 Müssen Sie jeden Tag üben? Wie lange?

4 Warum treiben Sie (keinen) Sport?

5 Wie oft gehen Sie ins Kino?

6 Was für Filme sehen Sie gern?

7 Was halten Sie von den neuesten Hits?

8 Was haben Sie gestern abend gemacht? Und am Samstag?

9 Was haben Sie heute abend vor? Und am Wochenende?

7 BASIC Reading

a) **NUR FÜR SCHWIMMER**

b) **Alle Badegäste tragen beim Schwimmen eine Bademütze**

c) **DUSCHE FÜR DAMEN**

d) **HERRENTOILETTE**

e) **BADEZEIT 1 STUNDE** einschließlich aus - und ankleiden

f) **BITTE NICHT HINEINSPRINGEN**

1 You would find these signs in a swimming pool. Give their English equivalents. ▶

FILMPROGRAMM JULI/AUGUST 1987

Messeschnellweg A 37 Abfahrt Kirchhorst

AUTO-KINO KIRCHHORST ▲▲▲

Mittwoch und Donnerstag: Familien-Kinotag! Pro Auto pro Vorstellung DM 12,–

Freitag und Samstag 0.15 Spätvorstellung

Kasse und Snackbar sind täglich ab 21.00 Uhr für Sie geöffnet!

täglich 22.00 Uhr

Rock & Rail: das Bahn- + Konzert -Ticket ab 89 Mark.

Rock & Rail. Das Musikereignis des Jahres. Die Königin der Pop-Musik live im Frankfurter Waldstadion. Am 22. August 1987 um 19 Uhr. Die Bahn macht's möglich, daß Madonna-Fans aus der ganzen Bundesrepublik an diesem Ereignis teilnehmen können. Mit dem Rock & Rail-Expreß. 20 Sonderzüge aus 25 Städten der Bundesrepublik bringen Sie nach Frankfurt.

Rock & Rail-Tickets gibt es ab 11. Juli bei allen Fahrkartenausgaben, DER-Reisebüros und den anderen Verkaufsagenturen der Bahn. Im Preis eingeschlossen sind Hin- und Rückfahrkarte und die Eintrittskarte zum Konzert.

Wer zu Madonna will, sollte schnellstens bestellen.

Das Konzert im Frankfurter Waldstadion ist das einzige in der Bundesrepublik.

MADONNA
WHO'S THAT GIRL WORLD TOUR 1987

SAMSTAG, 22. AUGUST BEGINN: 19 UHR FRANKFURT WALDSTADION

EINZIGES KONZERT IN DEUTSCHLAND!

VORVERKAUF: AB SAMSTAG, 11. JULI.

2 1 What is 'different' about this cinema?

2 If you drove there on a Thursday, how much would it cost for your parents, you and your two brothers?

3 When does the box-office open?

4 When do the films begin?

3 On holiday you hear that Madonna is performing in Germany. Your friend suggests you could go.

1 What is the likely cost?

2 What do you get for the price?

3 Give one place where tickets are on sale.

4 Why does your friend want to book the tickets this afternoon?

4 On the right is a summary of the main sports programmes on television this week.

1 What could you watch on Monday?

2 What choice of event is offered on Wednesday evening?

3 Which event is televised on Thursday?

4 What kind of Grand Prix could you watch on Friday?

5 What is taking place in Rome?

6 Which nations are competing in Saturday's other event?

> *ARD – Channel 1; ZDF – Channel 2;*
> *EM – Europameisterschaften;*
> *WM – Weltmeisterschaften*

Sport

Mo., 17.8.:	20.10 Uhr - ARD: Fußball-Länderspiel: Deutschland-Frankreich
Di., 18.8.:	23.00 Uhr - ARD: Schwimm-Europameister- schaften in Straßburg
Mi., 19.8.:	22.10 Uhr - ZDF: Fußball: 1. Bundesliga Schwimm-EM
Do., 20.8.:	14.15 Uhr - ARD: Rad-WM in Wien
Fr., 21.8.:	14.05 Uhr - ARD: Kanu-WM in Duisburg Motorrad-Grand-Prix von Italien
Sa., 22.8.:	14.05 Uhr - ARD: Leichtathletik-WM in Rom Schwimm-Länderkampf BRD-DDR

Unser Ausflug zum Vienenburger See

Papa wollte schon seinen Rucksack packen,
weil er eine zünftige Wanderung machen wollte.
Da hatte Mama eine ihrer besten Ideen. Wir
sollten doch mal mit dem Zug nach Vienenburg
fahren, an den See.

Kati sah den See zuerst, als wir in Vienenburg
ankamen. Ich wollte sfort zum Steg. Da sagte
aber Papa, „Erst gehn wir einmal um den See,
das tut uns allen gut." Einmal rum dauerte
ungefär eine dreiviertel Stunde. Die Grossen
schwärmten immerzu von der schönen Land=
schaft. Ich fand die Boote auf dem See viel
interesanter.

Endlich waren wir wieder an der Cafeteria.
Mama wollte Kaffee trinken. Kaffeetrinken ist
doch nichts für Kinder! Mama durfte also an
Land bleiben. Wir Männer und Kati haben uns
ein Ruderboot gemietet. Es war wirklich Spitze.
Die halbe Stunde war viel zu schnell vorüber.
Mama hatte inzwischen Kaffee getrunken.
Kati und ich machten uns über einen Riesen
Eisbecher her. Papa löschte seinen Durst mit
einem kühlen Bier. Eigentlich wollten Kati
und ich noch ein Elektroboot ausprobieren,
aber Papa fand, für heute ist's genug. Das
nächstemal dürfen wir Elektroboot fahren,
hat er gesagt.

◀ **5** 1 Where did the family go?

2 How did they get there?

3 What took them three quarters of an hour?

4 What did the rest of the family do whilst mother drank coffee?

5 What refreshments did father and the children choose?

6 What final treat did the children want?

Steg – landing stage

1 The local churches are organising holiday activities which you and your penfriend might take part in.

1 What has been arranged for Friday, July 3rd?

2 Where could you go on the Tuesday?

3 What might you need to borrow?

▶

Ferienaktionen für Jugendliche

BERENBOSTEL. Die Stephanus-Kirchengemeinde Berenbostel veranstaltet drei Ferienaktionen für Jugendliche ab 14 Jahren. Am Freitag, dem 3. Juli, startet um 22 Uhr eine Nachtwanderung durch den Deister; am Dienstag, dem 7. Juli, geht's um 9 Uhr los zum Steinhuder Meer per Fahrrad und am Freitag, dem 10. Juli, findet zusammen mit der Willehadi-Kirchengemeinde Garbsen eine Fahrt in den Heidepark nach Soltau statt (ab 12 J.).

◀

Wie meine Eltern ihre Freizeit verbringen

Manchmal kommt mein Vater schon um 16.30 Uhr von der Arbeit. Meistens hilft er dann meiner Mutter im Haushalt, so daß sich beide früher ausruhen können. An einigen Abenden im Monat ist nur mein Vater zu Hause, während meine Mutter zum Frauenkreis geht. An diesen Abenden sortiert mein Vater Briefmarken, liest Zeitung oder guckt Fernsehen. Manchmal ist aber auch er abends weg. Dann ist er zu einer Veranstaltung gefahren.

Einmal im Monat gehen meine Eltern ins Konzert. Sie haben ein Jahresabonnement. Für uns Kinder sind diese Abende immer schön, weil wir dann tun und lassen können, was wir wollen. An den meisten Wochenenden sind meine Eltern dann irgendwo eingeladen, oder haben selber Besuch. Diese Besuche gehen dann meistens bis 2.00 Uhr morgens. Manchmal, wenn meine Eltern nicht zu müde sind, gehen sie dann am Sonntagmorgen zum Gottesdienst, aber dies geschieht nur noch selten.

2

1 What does Antje's father often do when he comes home from work?

2 What does he do when he spends the evening alone at home?

3 How often do Antje's parents go to a concert?

4 What do the children feel about their parents going out in the evening?

5 Do her parents always go out together?

6 What kind of thing happens regularly at weekends?

7 Why are they often tired on Sundays?

2. MÜNDENER

CITYLAUF

"Rund um den Weserstein"

Ein Stadtlauf durch die historische
Altstadt, an drei Flüssen entlang
und über drei Brücken mit einem
großartigen Blick auf die

"ausgezeichnete Fachwerkstadt
Hann.-Münden"

an Werra, Fulda und Weser

Veranstaltungstag: S A M S T A G, 5. September 1987

Start und Ziel: An der St.Blasiuskirche in der Stadtmitte

Startgeld: Schüler und Jugendliche 1,--DM, Erwachsene 4,--DM

Allgemeine Hinweise:

Umkleide- und Duschmöglichkeiten: Im TG-Heim (50 Meter von Start und Ziel entfernt)
begrenzt vorhanden

Verpflegung: Bei schönem Wetter an Start/Ziel, sonst TG-Heim

Parkplätze: Ausreichend 300 Meter von Start/Ziel entfernt vorhanden

Der Veranstaltungstag ist ein 'langer Samstag'.
Die Veranstaltung findet bei jedem Wetter statt.

3 This event might appeal to some of your sport-minded family.

1 What activity is involved?

2 Where should participants assemble?

3 What are you told about the route?

4 Will the event be held if the weather is bad?

5 Where will you be able to park?

6 Are there any facilities for changing, etc?

7 What does *langer Samstag* tell you about the day of the event?

TG – *Turngemeinde – sports club*

4 On an exchange visit to Bochum you are shown this account of a concert that took place there recently.

1 Where was it held?

2 Who was the concert given by?

3 Who played 'Finlandia'?

4 What was Florian Schaller's role in this concert?

5 Why was this last item described as 'international'?

6 Would you say the concert was fairly good, quite enjoyable or a great success?

Musiker der Partnerstadt fügen sich problemlos ein
Fabelhaftes Konzert mit dem Jugendsinfonieorchester

Englisch-deutsche Partnerschaft in Vollendung konnte man in der Aula des Albert-Einstein-Gymnasiums erleben. Das "City of Sheffield Youth Orchestra" unter der Leitung von Julian Clayton war zu Gast in Bochum und gab – wie sollte es anders sein? – auch ein Gastkonzert! Die jungen Musiker spielten mit Mitgliedern des Jugendsinfonieorchesters der Musikschule Bochum, das bekanntlich von Guido van den Bosch geleitet wird, zusammen.

Sibelius' "Finlandia" op. 26, dieses zwar kurze, aber sehr wirkungsvolle Stück, musizierten beide Orchester gemeinsam. Guido van den Bosch lei-

tete das Ensemble, das sich ausgesprochen homogen und ausdrucksstark präsentierte.

Das Konzert für Violine und Orchester Nr. 1 von Max Bruch gestaltete das "City of Sheffield Youth Orchestra" unter der Leitung von Julian Clayton. Der Solist, Florian Schaller, Jahrgang 1968, ist der 1. Konzertmeister des Jugendsinfonieorchesters. Auch diese Leistung war bewundernswert. Die Interpretation des Bruch-Konzertes setzte die Hörer in Erstaunen und forderte frenetischen Beifall heraus. Das Orchester begleitete souverän und klangschön, so daß auch diese internationale Darbietung glänzend gelang.

7
BASIC
Writing

1 Your penfriend has asked what leisure facilities there are in your area. Make a list in German of what there is to do, e.g. zwei Kinos.

Freizeitangebot bei uns in.....
1
2
3
4
5
6

2 Your class are going to correspond as individuals with a class in the Carl-Duisburg-Gymnasium in Wuppertal. The Wuppertal teacher will be making the pairings. She has asked you all to write in German a few sentences about your hobbies and how you spend your spare time so she can find someone with similar interests.

3 Your exchange visit to Germany is proving very hectic. You have been there a week and so far you have done something different every day. You are keeping a brief diary of the main things you did. Bring your diary up to date. The first entry has been done for you.

SONNTAG   Heute waren wir im Zoo
MONTAG
DIENSTAG
MITTWOCH
DONNERSTAG
FREITAG
SAMSTAG

1 You have recently been on an exchange visit to Innsbruck. The British and Austrian schools are producing scrap books to send to each other to encourage next year's pupils to take part. Write a paragraph in German (about 100 words long) describing how you spent the day that you enjoyed most of all.

2 You and your mother are hoping to spend the next summer holiday in Germany, possibly near Freiburg in the Black Forest. Write a letter of about 100 words to the tourist office (Verkehrsamt) in Freiburg, the largest town in the area.

– Explain which activities you both enjoy.

– Enquire about facilities for these and ask if they have leaflets listing charges, opening times etc.

– Ask them to send you lists of accommodation and details of what is on in the area at the time of your visit.

3 Write a short description of these people and say what they are doing.

8 BASIC Listening

Banks, post and telephones

1 You will hear four customers in the post office. The recording was made in sections. You will hear each section twice. Then answer the questions.

Section 1

1 What two things does the woman ask the price of?

Section 2

2 Why has the man come to the post office?

3 Does he get what he came for?

Section 3

4 What is this customer doing?

5 How much does it cost?

Section 4

6 How many stamps does this woman buy?

7 What else does she want to do?

8 Where can she do it?

2 You will hear a man telling a child how to do something. You will hear the instructions twice. What is the child being taught to do?

3 You will hear a man buying something from a kiosk. You will hear the conversation twice.

– What does the man buy?

– What country is he in?

4 You will hear two people asking questions in the street. The tape was recorded in sections. You will hear each section twice.

Section 1

What does the woman want to do?

Which two possibilities are there?

Section 2

What does the man want to do?

Where does the woman send him?

5 You will hear a man asking about post office opening hours. You will hear the conversation twice.

1 What time does the post office open on weekdays?

2 What time does it open on Saturdays?

3 What time does the office close on weekdays?

4 What time does it close on Saturdays?

1 You will hear a man having trouble making a phone call. Why does he not get through? You will hear the conversation twice.

2 You will hear a customer at a bank. The tape is in sections. You will hear each section twice. Listen and then answer the questions.

Section 1

1 What does the customer want to do?

2 What does the clerk want to see?

3 What question does the customer ask?

Section 2

4 What does the clerk ask the customer to do?

5 Why should the customer go over to the left?

3 You will hear a woman speaking to a man in the street. Listen carefully and then answer the questions below. You will hear the conversation twice.

1 What has she got?

2 What does she want?

3 Why does she need it?

4 A visitor is asking for help in the tourist office. You will hear the dialogue twice.

1 What is the tourist's problem?

2 Why can't he use the cash dispenser?

3 What else could he try?

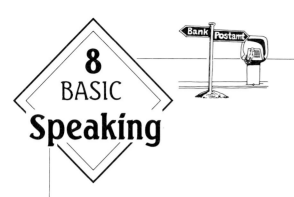

8
BASIC
Speaking

1 Work in pairs, one of you asking the questions, the other giving directions. Take it in turns to play each part.

EXCHANGE PUPIL	HOST
Ask where you can change money.	Explain where there is a bank.
Ask if it is open this afternoon.	Say yes, until 4pm.
Ask where you can buy stamps.	Say in the post office.
Ask where that is.	Explain.
Ask where the nearest post-box is.	Explain.
Ask if you may phone your parents.	Say that your phone is out of order.
Ask where there is a public phone.	Explain.

2 Work in pairs. Take it in turns to play each part.

CUSTOMER	POST OFFICE CLERK
Ask the cost of a postcard to your country.	Give the price.
Buy five stamps at that price.	Ask if he/she wants anything else.
Say you'd like to make a phone call.	Say box number one is free.
Thank the clerk and ask where to pay.	Say he/she must pay at this counter.

BANK CLERK	CUSTOMER
Greet your customer.	Say you'd like to change a DM 50 note.
Ask if he/she would like two DM 20 and one DM 10 notes.	Say you would prefer four DM 10 notes and some coins.
Ask what coins he/she would like.	Say one DM 5, two DM 2 and one DM 1.
Count out the money, and say the total.	

FRIEND 1	FRIEND 2
Ask if your exchange partner has a telephone at home.	Say yes, and give your number (29 31).
Ask what the dialling code is.	Tell your friend it is 0845.
Ask if he/she would like your number.	Say yes, please.
Give your number; it is 607331, and the code is 0246.	Repeat the numbers.

1 Your penfriend is meeting his friends in town. He suggests phoning when he is ready for a lift home. He has asked you how to use a call box.

- Tell him where there is a phone box in the town centre.

- Explain that you lift the receiver.

- You dial the number – you don't need any dialling code.

- When you hear someone answer, you put in a 10p piece.

- He shouldn't need more money than that.

- Remind him of your phone number.

- Ask him if he understands.

2 Work in pairs. Take it in turns to play each part.

VISITOR	HOST
Ask if you may make a phone call.	Say of course.
Ask for the Hamburg phone directory.	Apologise, because you don't have one.
Ask how you ring directory enquiries.	Say the number is 0 11 88.

VISITOR	CORINNA'S BROTHER
Dial the Hamburg code (40) and the number you want (7 50 33) out loud.	Answer the phone; give your surname – Schnabel.
Ask to speak to Corinna.	Say she's not there at the moment.
Ask if she will be in this evening.	Say you think so.
Arrange for Corinna to ring you back. Give your penfriend's number (Osterwald 78 85).	Say you'll tell Corinna to ring Osterwald 78 85 this evening.

3 Work in pairs. Take it in turns to play each each part.

CUSTOMER	BANK CLERK
Ask if you can cash a traveller's cheque at this counter.	Ja, würden Sie bitte den Scheck unterschreiben.
Ask for a pen.	(Hand it over.) Bitte schön. Darf ich bitte Ihren Ausweis haben?
(Hand it over.) Ask what today's exchange rate is.	Das Pfund steht heute bei zwei Komma drei Franken
Ask what the fee is.	Für einen Scheck nehmen wir fünf Franken. Sie bekommen also 41 Franken.

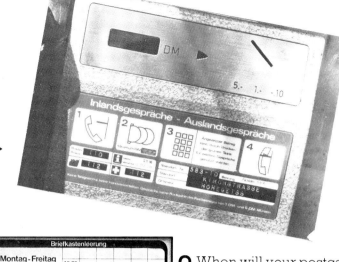

1 1 What calls can you make from this phone?

2 Which coins does it accept?

2 What don't you need if you want to phone from here?

Briefkastenleerung			
Montag - Freitag	16.30		
Samstag	11.30		
Sonntag	8.00		

Nächste Leerung   Mittwoch

3 When will your postcards be collected from this box?

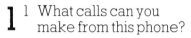

Telefonieren ohne Münzen

Karten-Telefon

National · International

⚡ Post

4 At the post office you need to buy stamps and phone your home in Wales. Is it better to queue at counter 1 or 2?

1 Postwertzeichen
Sondermarken
Wert- und Einschreibsendungen
Ferngespräche Telegramme
Briefausgabe
Wechselsteuermarken

2 Einzahlungen In- und Ausland
Postsparkasse
Postbarschecks
Postwertzeichen in kleinen Mengen

Lassen Sie nie eurocheques und
eurocheque-Karte im Wagen liegen.
Jeder Scheck hat einen Wert von 400 DM.

5 This leaflet appeared on the windscreen whilst your car was parked. What is its message?

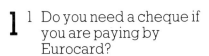

1 1 Do you need a cheque if you are paying by Eurocard?

2 What do you need to do?

3 Give six places which accept Eurocard.

▶

Mit EUROCARD bezahlen Sie einfach und bequem, nur mit Ihrer Unterschrift.

Ohne Bargeld, ohne Scheck – nur Karte vorlegen und Beleg unterschreiben; so einfach bezahlen Sie mit EUROCARD. In angeschlossenen Hotels, Restaurants, Kaufhäusern, Autowerkstätten, Fachgeschäften aller Branchen und bei nahezu allen Fluggesellschaften und Autovermietungen. Im In- und Ausland.

TELEFON-KARTE
Telefonieren ohne Münzen
40 Einheiten
Deutsche Bundespost

...Karten, mit denen Sie telefonieren können. Damit sind Sie endlich unabhängig vom Kleingeld. Sie müssen Gespräche nicht abbrechen, weil Sie keine Münzen mehr haben, und Sie können sich ganz auf Ihr Gespräch konzentrieren, ohne den Münzenvorrat zu beobachten. Telefon-Karten gibt es mit 40 oder 80 Einheiten zum Preis von 12,– DM bzw. 24,– DM.

REISEGELD FÜR ALLE WELT

GELDWECHSEL
EXCHANGE - CAMBIO
...auch Samstag, Sonntag und nach Feierabend

Bargeld gegen ▣ und Kreditkarten.
Rund um die Uhr: Geldautomaten.
DEUTSCHE VERKEHRS-KREDIT-BANK

München – Flughafen
täglich 7.00 – 22.00 Uhr
Telefon 90 61 10

München-Hauptbahnhof
täglich 6.00 – 23.30 Uhr
Telefon 1 26 08–37

▲

2 1 What is being advertised here?

2 What are said to be its advantages?

▲

3 Your flight has been delayed by fog. You arrive at Munich airport at 9.30pm on Friday without enough cash for the weekend.

1 How much time is there to find the airport bank before it closes?

2 What banking facilities are there at weekends in the town centre?

Wichtige Postämter

Postamt 32, Bahnhofplatz 1, M 2   Tel. 53 88-27 32
Täglich 0--24 Uhr – Öffentliche Telexstelle täglich 7--23 Uhr. Alle unter »hauptpostlagernd« eingehenden Sendungen werden beim Postamt 32 zur Abholung bereitgehalten. Postsparkassendienst, Auszahlung von Schecks und Geldwechsel auch nachts. Öffentliches Schreibtelefon für Gehörlose. Keine Annahme von Paketen und Wertsendungen.

Postamt 1, Residenzstraße 2, M 2   Tel. 53 88-25 10/25 11
Mo mit Fr 8–18, Frühschalter 7–8, Spätschalter 18–18.30, Sa 8–12 Uhr, Frühschalter 7–8, Spätschalter 12–13 Uhr, So u. Fei geschlossen. Geldwechsel.

Postamt 31, Bahnhofplatz 2, M 2   Tel. 53 88-27 20/27 22
(im Hauptbahnhof)
Mo mit Fr 7–21, Sa 8–21 Uhr, So u. Fei geschlossen.

◀ **4** 1 Which post offices accept parcels?

2 Your GCSE results were sent to Munich *poste restante*. Where can you collect them?

3 When does Post Office 32 close?

4 At which post offices could you obtain foreign currency?

8
BASIC
Writing

1 Note down in German some useful information for your exchange partner who will be arriving soon. You have found out that the post office is open from 9am to 5.30pm (closed 12.30–1.30 for lunch), the bank opens at 10am and closes at 3pm. To phone Germany you dial 010 49, then the area code, then the number you want; cheap rates are from 8pm to 8am and at weekends.

2 When you arrive home after your holiday in Germany you discover that the present you sent for your grandparents' Golden Wedding anniversary has not arrived. Write to the post office in Landsberg making the following points:

- You posted a parcel there on August 2nd.

- It has not arrived.

- Say what it contained.

- Say that you have the receipt for the parcel (die Paketkarte).

- Give the number that is on the receipt.

- Ask if they can help you.

Das Postamt.
Schalterstunden:

Der nächste Briefkasten

Ein Brief nach
Deutschland kostet:

Wo kauft man
Postkarten?

Wie telefoniert man
mit Deutschland?

Wann telefoniert
man am billigsten?

Geld wechseln/
Reiseschecks einlösen
– wo?

Bank – Schalterstunden:

1 Describe what is happening in this picture, using these questions as a guide.

1. Wo sind diese Leute?
2. Wer wird schon bedient?
3. Wo gibt man Pakete auf?
4. Wer holt ein Paket ab?
5. Wer kauft wahrscheinlich Briefmarken?
6. Was macht der kleine Junge?
7. Was kann man in der Ecke hinter der Glastür machen?
8. An welchem Schalter muß man das bezahlen?
9. Beschreiben Sie den Mann, der am Tisch sitzt.
10. Was macht er?

2 Study the pictures, then tell the story in German, using about 100 words.

Everyday problems

1 You have cut your foot and have gone to the chemist for a large dressing. You will hear each section of the tape twice. Listen carefully, then answer the questions.

Section 1

1 What does she say about the cut?

2 What does she suggest you should do?

Section 2

3 When would be the best time?

4 How will you find the place?

2 The radio is broadcasting an urgent message for Herr Kornstedt from Lauenstein. You will hear the message twice.

– What is Herr Kornstedt asked to do?

3 A woman has gone to the lost property office. You will hear the conversation twice.

– What has she lost?

– Where did she lose it?

– Have they got it?

4 You are listening to the car radio. The 8 o'clock traffic bulletin begins with a warning. You will hear it twice.

– What is the problem?

– Which part of the country is affected?

1 You will hear a motorist talking on a roadside emergency phone. The tape is in sections. You will hear each section twice.

Section 1

1 What kind of road is the motorist on?

2 Which direction is he travelling in?

Section 2

3 What is wrong?

4 What seems to be the cause?

2 You will hear a news item from West German radio. Listen and then answer the questions below. You will hear each section twice.

Section 1

1 What is the report about?

2 What casualties were there?

Section 2

3 Who was to blame, according to the report?

4 What were the motorcyclists doing when the incident happened?

3 You will hear Frau Greiner making a telephone call. The tape is in sections. You will hear each one twice.

Section 1

1 Who has Frau Greiner rung?

2 What does she want?

3 When was she last there?

Section 2

4 Which day would she prefer?

5 Does Frau Greiner choose an earlier or later time than is first suggested?

9 BASIC Speaking

1 On holiday in Germany you fall ill. Work in pairs. Take it in turns to tell your host what is the matter.

HOST	YOU
Was möchtest du heute morgen essen?	Say nothing, thanks
Geht es dir nicht gut?	Say no. You have a stomach-ache/headache.
Seit wann?	Say since Tuesday/yesterday evening.
Ist es schlimm?	Say yes, very. You'd like to go to bed/see a doctor, please.
Ich rufe gleich bei Doktor Tamm an.	

2 When you were alone in the house this afternoon you had to take a phone message from your host, Herr Rekowski. You wrote it down in English, but when Frau Rekowski returns you have to tell her in German what has happened. This is what you wrote:

Mr. R. Rang 3.50
near Frankfurt –
car broken down
home VERY late
will ring again about
9.00 pm

3 Explain to your friend that you have lost a pullover. Work in pairs, taking turns to play each part.

YOU	FRIEND
Say you have lost your pullover.	Ask which one. The blue one?
Say no, the white one.	Ask when he/she lost it.
Say probably yesterday.	Ask where.
Say you don't know. Perhaps in the woods or by the river.	Say you don't think so. Your friend had the pullover in the cake shop.
Say perhaps it is still there. Suggest you phone to ask.	Say that is a good idea! Why don't you do it straight away?

4 Work in pairs, taking turns to ask and answer the questions.

INTERVIEWER	STUDENT
Wie geht es Ihnen heute?	OK/great!/awful!
Sind Sie oft krank?	Never/hardly ever/very often.
Fehlen Sie oft in der Schule?	About once a year/every Friday/only in winter.
Wie oft waren Sie schon im Krankenhaus?	Once/three times/too often!
Haben Sie Angst vor dem Zahnarzt?	Not at all/sometimes/yes, terribly!
Haben Sie diese Woche Tabletten genommen?	No/not this week/yes, for earache.
Wann waren Sie das letzte Mal beim Zahnarzt?	Last week/don't know/a long time ago.

1 It is your last day in Germany and you have lots to do. Work in pairs. Take it in turns to play each part.

PHOTOGRAPHER'S ASSISTANT	YOU
Guten Morgen. Was darf es sein?	Say you'd like to collect your photographs.
Auf welchen Namen?	Tell him/her.
Wann haben Sie den Film gebracht?	Say two days ago.
Es tut mir leid, sie sind noch nicht da.	Ask if they will be there before half past two.
Ja, ich glaube schon.	Say you hope so!

TOYSHOP ASSISTANT	YOU
Guten Morgen. Bitte schön?	Say you bought this toy yesterday but it won't work.
Das dürfte nicht sein. Da ist etwas bestimmt nicht in Ordnung.	Ask if you may exchange it.
Gerne, wenn Sie die Quittung haben.	Say you've left it in the hotel.
Ohne Quittung kann ich Ihnen leider nicht helfen.	Say that's a pity. You will have to come back this afternoon.

YOU	JEWELLER
Say your watch is not working. It might need a new battery.	Ask to see it. Say he/she is right.
Ask if the jeweller can fit one.	Say of course you can.
Ask when it will be ready.	Say in about a quarter of an hour.
Ask if you should pay now.	Say no, that's not necessary.

YOU	LOST-PROPERTY OFFICIAL
Say you have lost a shopping bag.	Ask when and where it was lost.
Say this morning between 8 and 9, in the tram/bus.	Ask if the bag was made of leather.
Say no, plastic.	Ask if this is the person's bag.
Say yes, that's it!	Ask what was in the bag.
Say a map of the town, your sunglasses, a cassette player, a can of coke and your passport.	Say this is definitely his/her bag!
Say how pleased you are to have it back again.	

2 The friend you are youth hostelling with has been awake all night with toothache. Ask the hostel warden the following:

a) Is there a dentist in the village?

b) What is the best way to get there?

c) Is it far?

d) What are his surgery hours?

e) Should you telephone beforehand?

f) What is his telephone number?

g) Where is the telephone?

9
BASIC
Reading

1 A bottle of sun-tan oil has spilled inside your friend's suitcase. What would it cost her to have each of these items cleaned?

a) a dress
b) a skirt
c) a pair of trousers

Unsere Preise	
Vollreinigung	
Pulli	2.95
Rock	4.60
Hose	4.70
Jacke	5.90
Kleid	5.90
Mantel (Wolle)	8.90

2 You have been helping unload some goods at the supermarket run by your penfriend's family. Why was Herr Meyer so cross when you stacked the boxes in front of this notice?

Notausgang
bitte freihalten

4 1 What happens if you dial 112?
2 What three pieces of information should you be ready to give?

In jedem Fall gilt bei einem Brand:

Die Feuerwehr verständigen

Notruf 112

Bei der Meldung angeben:
- Wer ruft an
- Was ist passiert
- Wo ist das Schadensereignis

3 Your father has been awake all night with toothache, your sister's eyes are red and itchy.

1 Who should Dad consult?
2 Who should your sister consult?

Rechtsanwalt u. Notar

Dr. med. Reinke
Augenarzt

Dr. Heidi Reinke
Zahnärztin

Dr. med. S. Dinkel
Arzt

5 You and your exchange partner are exploring a half-built house when a passer-by draws your attention to this sign.

- What does it say?
- Who might get into trouble if you take no notice?

Betreten der Baustelle verboten!
Eltern haften für ihre Kinder

1 The family car has broken down on the motorway. You have gone with your mother to the emergency phone.

- What should you do to operate this equipment?
- Should you speak first?

▶

Notruf
Klappe hochheben und festhalten! Warten bis Autobahnmeisterei sich meldet!

2 You have been prescribed some pills (Dragees) for an itchy rash.

- How many should you take?
- When should you take them?

Dosierung und Anwendungsweise:
Falls vom Arzt nicht anders verordnet, gelten folgende Dosierungsrichtlinien:

Erwachsene und Kinder	2 bis 6 Dragees pro Tag
über 10 Jahre	2 bis 4 Dragees pro Tag
von 5 bis 10 Jahren.	1 bis 3 Dragees pro Tag
von 2 bis 5 Jahren.	1 bis 2 Dragees pro Tag
bis 2 Jahre.	

Die Tagesdosis wird in mehrere Einzeldosen unterteilt.
Die Dragees sollen unzerkaut während oder kurz nach den Mahlzeiten eingenommen werden.

Zwölfjähriger Autofahrer verursacht schweren Unfall

ebb. **Goslar**

Mit dem Auto seines Vaters, eines Polizeibeamten, hat ein Zwölfjähriger aus Liebenburg (Kreis Goslar) in der Nacht zum Sonnabend eine folgenschwere Spritztour unternommen. Der Schüler und sein zwei Jahre älterer Beifahrer erlitten bei einem Unfall nach einer Verfolgungsjagd mit der Polizei lebensgefährliche Verletzungen. Gegen 2.30 Uhr beobachteten Beamte einer Funkstreife, wie das Auto mit hoher Geschwindigkeit bei Rot über eine Kreuzung in der Goslarer Innenstadt fuhr und nahmen die Verfolgung auf. In einer scharfen Rechtskurve fuhr der Zwölfjährige geradeaus, raste über einen Fußweg und einen Grünstreifen und prallte gegen eine Mauer. Die beiden Jungen kamen mit schweren Verletzungen ins Krankenhaus, das Auto wurde total zerstört. Die Polizei untersucht jetzt, wie der Schüler an die Wagenschlüssel kommen konnte.

3 You hear that there has been a serious accident near your hotel. Some days later this report of the crash appears in the paper.

1 Who was driving the car?

2 Who else was in the car?

3 Where was the car when the police first noticed it?

4 How was it being driven?

5 Describe the scene of the accident, and how the car came to crash.

6 What was the damage to a) the car? b) the occupants?

7 What are the police trying to discover?

9 BASIC Writing

1 Write a note to your penfriend.

- Wish him/her a merry Christmas and ask how he/she is.

- Say you have a cold and a sore throat, but your mother is better, thank goodness. You don't enjoy helping round the house.

- Tell him/her that your exams begin on Thursday. You will write a long letter in January.

2 Unpacking at a new hotel the family notices that several things are missing – an umbrella, a camera, a street map, a bag of sweets, two cassette tapes, a swim-suit, 5 or 6 picture postcards and an expensive biro. They were all in a small black bag. You might have left it at the swimming pool, in the last hotel, in a café, or you might even have lost it in town. A German friend volunteers to phone round on your behalf, but he needs a list of the missing objects. Write one in German, adding further details (size, colour, make etc) as appropriate.

3 Your German visitor Moritz is totally deaf. He has fallen ill and lost his voice. The doctor said Moritz must stay in bed for two days. He has to take two tablets three times a day before meals. He must also drink plenty of water or fruit juice but he must avoid alcohol. Moritz has not under-stood the instructions. He hands you this note. Answer his questions.

> Wann darf ich aufstehen?
> Wie oft soll ich die Tabletten nehmen?
> Wann soll ich sie nehmen?
> Soll ich nur eine Tablette nehmen?
> Was darf ich (nicht) trinken?

1 Study this letter from the boy you exchanged with last year. Write a reply telling him:

- You're sorry he can't come and that his father is still out of work; lots of people in this country have the same problem.

- You got details of a new exchange partner today – from the same school as Volker; perhaps you will meet again after all.

- You can't do any sport just now; last week you fell off your bike and broke your leg.

- It was fun doing nothing at first, but now you're bored.

- Ask Volker to write again soon.

> Cham, dem 4. Januar
>
> Lieber Simon!
>
> Vielen Dank für Deinen Brief. Leider darf ich dieses Jahr nicht am Austausch teilnehmen. Ich habe Dir schon erzählt, mein Vater ist seit Ende Juli arbeitslos und hat immer noch keine Hoffnung auf eine neue Stelle hier in Cham. Wir fahren also wahrscheinlich gar nicht in Urlaub. Ich bin ja mächtig enttäuscht, aber da ist einfach nichts zu machen.
> Wie geht es Dir? Habt Ihr auch so viel Schnee wie wir? Ich fahre fast jeden Tag Ski!
> Alles Gute, auch an Deine Familie,
>
> Dein Volker

2 You are about to leave for home when you see this advert. It is the wrong time of day to phone, but the receptionist at your hotel suggests you write an account of what you saw, giving your name, home address and phone number. She will phone the advertiser and pass on your report. This is what you saw:

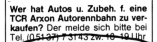

Wer hat Autos u. Zubeh. f. eine TCR Arxon Autorennbahn zu verkaufen? Der melde sich bitte bei Tel. (05137) 73143 zw. 18–19 Uhr

Unfallzeugen gesucht! Wer hat den Unfall am Planetenring am Mittw., den 30. 9. 87 um 19 Uhr beobachtet. Bitte dringend sich zu melden! Tel. (0511) 661957 von 7.30–16.00 Uhr

Unterstellmöglichkeit f. 1 Büfett gesucht. Höhe 2,80, Tiefe 0,60, Breite 3 m, Tel. (0511) 757568

Ich mache saubere Tapezierarbeiten. Tel. (0511) 712656

Su. **Nachhilfe** i. Mathe f. 8. Kl. Gymn. Tel. (0511) 407730 ab 18 Uhr

Future plans and employment

1 On this tape five people are talking about their jobs. You will hear each person twice. Decide which of the three jobs they do.

1st person

a) writer
b) secretary
c) receptionist

2nd person

a) petrol pump attendant
b) car salesman
c) car mechanic

3rd person

a) shop assistant
b) disc-jockey
c) pop singer

4th person

a) nurse
b) kindergarten teacher
c) waitress

5th person

a) architect
b) farmer
c) builder

2 In your hotel a woman is on holiday with three young children. You overhear her explaining her plans to a friend. You will hear the extract twice.

1 Who will be joining her?

2 When will the person arrive?

3 How long will they spend on holiday together?

3 You are listening to the radio when you catch the name of Princess Diana. You will hear each section twice.

Section 1

Which town is she to visit?

What is everyone keen to know?

Section 2

Who will be wearing a grey blazer, black skirt and grey shoes?

4 On the radio the announcer is telling listeners about programmes to be broadcast later in the day. The tape is in sections. Listen and then answer the questions. You will hear each section twice.

Section 1

You're keen to hear the result of an international football match. What time is the early evening sports programme?

Section 2

You like to fall asleep with the radio on. Which of these programmes begins at 11.10pm?

a) book review

b) the life-stories of famous composers

c) classical piano music

d) a concert from the Schleswig–Holstein music festival.

1 A German woman is talking about her holiday plans. The tape is in sections. You will hear each section twice.

Section 1

1 Where would they like to go?

2 When are they hoping to get there?

Section 2

3 What plans for this summer came to nothing?

4 What kind of sport is mentioned?

2 Marlies, Stefan and Sven are looking for holiday jobs. You will hear them being interviewed by their prospective employers. Copy and complete the grid below. You will hear each interview twice.

		Where will they work?	Two things they must do	What is the pay?	What are the hours?
1	Marlies				
2	Stefan				
3	Sven				

3 Listen to Daniela talking about her plans for the future. You will hear the item twice.

1 What will she be doing next year?

2 What does she think about the possibility of becoming a doctor?

3 Which career would be her second choice?

4 You are spending the Whit holiday at an international youth camp. You have just invited four German friends to visit you during the summer. Copy the grid into your exercise book and fill in the information about each of their holiday plans. You will hear the recording twice.

	Where	Date/time	Who with	Accommodation
Kerstin				
Oliver				
Sonja				
Julia				

10 BASIC Speaking

1 Answer these questions; work in pairs.

1 Wann bist du mit der Schule fertig?
2 Was möchtest du später werden?
3 Warum?
4 In welcher Stadt möchtest du arbeiten?
5 Ist es leicht, in dieser Stadt eine Arbeit zu finden?
6 Wer arbeitet in einem Krankenhaus?
7 Wo arbeitet eine Sekretärin?
8 Wer bringt dir Post von deiner Brieffreundin?
9 Was macht ein Pilot?
10 Wer bringt dir das Essen in einem Restaurant?

2 You and your father have been discussing what you might do during your penfriend's visit. You made these rough notes. Tell your penfriend what you have planned. (Jo is your best friend.)

Sun   –   Seaside by car
Mon   am – table tennis
       pm – museum
Tues   am – ??
       pm – Jo's house for tea and T.V.
Wed   –   Shopping
       evening – Anita's party
Thurs –   bus trip to York or Chester
Fri   –   ?
            8pm disco
Sat   –   shopping
            evening – barbecue or cinema

3 Work in pairs. Take turns to ask and answer these questions:

1 Wieviel Taschengeld bekommst du pro Woche?
2 Ist das genug?
3 Was machst du mit dem Geld?
4 Sparst du etwas von deinem Taschengeld?
5 Wenn ja: Auf was sparst du?
   Wenn nein: Warum sparst du nicht?
6 Mußt du mit dem Geld Kleider kaufen?
7 Möchtest du gerne einen Job haben?
8 Wenn ja: Wann möchtest du arbeiten?
   Wenn nein: Warum nicht?
9 Was für Jobs gibt es in dieser Stadt?
10 Ist es leicht, so einen Job zu bekommen?

1 Your diary for the summer looks like this:

Answer these questions. Work in pairs.

1 Was hast du zu Pfingsten vor?

2 Wann beginnen die Prüfungen?

3 Wie lange dauern sie?

4 Wieviele Prüfungen machst du?

5 Wann erfährst du, welche Noten du bekommen hast?

6 Was hast du nach den Prüfungen vor?

7 Am wievielten ist die Schule zu Ende?

8 Wann geht die Schule im Herbst wieder los?

9 Fährst du mit deinen Eltern in Urlaub?

10 Wohin fährst du und mit wem?

11 Wo verbringst du den Rest deiner Ferien?

12 Und was hast du im September vor?

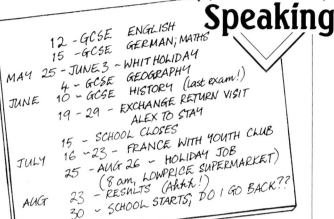

MAY 12 - GCSE ENGLISH
15 - GCSE GERMAN; MATHS
25 - JUNE 3 ~ WHIT HOLIDAY
JUNE 4 - GCSE GEOGRAPHY
10 - GCSE HISTORY (last exam!)
19 - 29 - EXCHANGE RETURN VISIT ALEX TO STAY
JULY 15 - SCHOOL CLOSES
16 - 23 - FRANCE WITH YOUTH CLUB
25 - AUG 26 - HOLIDAY JOB (8 am, LOWPRICE SUPERMARKET)
AUG 23 - RESULTS (Ahhh!)
30 ~ SCHOOL STARTS; DO I GO BACK??

2 On holiday in Austria you've made friends with some local people. They are keen to find out about your family and ask about their jobs. Because you don't know the German name for their jobs, you have to describe what they do.

– Your father is a long-distance lorry driver.

– Your mother teaches sewing in evening classes.

– Your brother is learning to be a car mechanic.

– Your grandmother runs the village post office.

– You hope to become a hotel receptionist.

3 Work in pairs. Answer these questions:

1 Werden Sie später studieren?

2 Wenn ja: Was möchten Sie studieren, und warum?

Wenn nein: Was für eine Arbeitsstelle werden Sie suchen?

3 Haben Sie schon einen Job?

4 Wenn ja: Was machen Sie? Wann arbeiten Sie? Bekommen Sie viel Geld?

Wenn nein: Warum arbeiten Sie nicht?

5 Gibt es in Ihrer Stadt viele Arbeitslose?

6 Möchten Sie in einer anderen Stadt arbeiten? Warum (nicht)?

7 Bekommen Sie genug Taschengeld?

8 Was würden Sie machen, wenn Sie keine Arbeitsstelle und daher viel Freizeit hätten?

9 Was ist Ihr Traumberuf? Wo möchten Sie am allerliebsten arbeiten?

10 Würden Sie arbeiten, wenn Sie sehr reich wären? Wo? Als was? Warum (nicht)?

10 BASIC Reading

1 Pupils around the world were asked by a German magazine how they saw the future.

1 What does Gunnar think everyone will have?

2 What will Walter do with his time?

3 What problem does Corinne foresee?

4 Where does the Turkish writer think things should be different?

5 What two changes does he/she think might happen?

SCHULE AUSBILDUNG BERUF

„Es gibt keine Arbeitslosigkeit, weil alle Menschen arbeiten müssen, um die Maschinen zu ersetzen."
Gunnar (15), Dänemark

„Ich habe viel Zeit für die Kinder, weil ich nur zehn Stunden in der Woche arbeite."
Walter Schelten, Holland

„Ich glaube, es werden sehr viele arbeitslos. Roboter werden die Arbeit machen."
Corinne (12), Luxemburg

„Es würden in den Schulen vielleicht Roboter anstatt Lehrer da sein, und sie würden Beispiele nicht an der Tafel zeigen, sondern auf Videos."
Türkei

---

2 Read these articles about holiday jobs, and answer the questions.

GUTEN ABEND, DORT ENTLANG

Carsten, 19 Jahre alt und Schüler in Mainz, hat einen Job als Kontrolleur im Kino. Einmal in der Woche arbeitet er elf Stunden am Stück, ab 12 Uhr mittags. „Eintrittskarten kontrollieren ist nicht anstrengend. Und außerdem kann ich in den Pausen sogar noch für das Abitur lernen", meint Carsten. Beruflich hat er mit dem Kino nichts im Sinn. Er will Mathematik und Physik studieren. Das Geld braucht Carsten, der noch bei seinen Eltern wohnt, für sein Auto.

BURGER UND POMMES

So einfach kann das gehen: „Ich habe gefragt, ob was frei ist, und die haben gesagt, okay, fang bei uns an." Das war vor fünf Jahren. Seitdem arbeitet Margarete (23) bei McDonalds.
Margarete studiert Geologie. Sie muß jobben, weil ihre Fahrten in ferne Länder viel Geld kosten. „Wir sind hier ein ganz lustiges Team, vor allem Schüler und Hausfrauen. Vier an der Kasse, vier in der Küche. Am Mittag und am frühen Abend ist viel los, aber sonst ist die Arbeit recht locker. Und das Essen ist frei."

3 A church service (Gottesdienst) is to be held on August 10th.

1 Who is it for?

2 Who else can go?

3 What time does it start?

4 What is planned for afterwards?

---

1 Where does Carsten work?

2 What hours does he work?

3 What is his job?

4 Does Carsten still attend school?

5 What are his plans for the future?

6 How does he use the money he earns?

7 How long has Margarete been working at McDonalds?

8 What is her main occupation?

9 Why does she need the money?

10 What sort of people work with her?

11 What two jobs need doing at McDonalds?

12 Which are the busiest times of day?

13 What 'perk' does Margarete get?

Gottesdienst für Schulanfänger

GARBSEN. Die ev.-luth. Willehadi-Kirchengemeinde lädt die Schulanfänger und ihre Eltern und Angehörigen ein zu einem Schulanfängergottesdienst am Montag, 10. August, 15 Uhr.

Nach dem Gottesdienst sind die kleinen ABC-Schützen mit ihren Angehörigen eingeladen zu Kaffee und Kuchen und zum Spielen und Basteln im Gemeindesaal, oder – wenn es schönes Wetter ist – auf dem Kirchplatz.

Read each passage, then answer the questions.

1
1 How easy is it to find a good part-time job?

2 What do most people use the money for?

3 Why are a few 'jobbers' particularly fortunate?

4 How much can young people expect to earn?

5 What do most people think of their jobs?

2
1 When does Silke work?

2 What is her job?

3 Where can she be seen?

4 How easy is it to get work?

5 How does she feel about making this job into a full-time career?

Zehn Mark die Stunde

Ferienzeit, freie Zeit? – Für viele Schüler und Studenten nicht. Fast jeder hat schon einmal so einen Job gehabt, als Zeitungsjunge, Babysitter . . . , aber es wird immer schwieriger, eine gute Teilzeitarbeit zu bekommen.

Die meisten jobben, um sich ein paar Extras leisten zu können: Urlaub, Auto, Stereoanlage. Ganz wenige haben Glück und können sich mit dem Nebenjob auf den späteren Beruf vorbereiten. Der Lohn für Ferienarbeit liegt heute zwischen 7 und 15 Mark pro Stunde. Wer noch keine 15 Jahre alt ist, darf nur in besonderen Ausnahmefällen eine Arbeit annehmen. Auch wenn es manchmal sehr hart ist und fast die ganze Freizeit dabei verlorengeht – alle Jobber, die wir besuchten, waren zufrieden und behaupteten: Jobben macht Spaß!

BITTE RECHT FREUNDLICH!

Privat trägt Silke (16, Schülerin) Jeans und Sweatshirt, kümmert sich um ihre fünf Katzen und geht am Wochenende gern in die Disco. Ein ganz „normales" Mädchen also. In den Schulferien aber schlüpft Silke in eine andere Haut. Silke jobt als Fotomodell und Mannequin.

Das Geschäft geht gut: Junge Fotomodelle für Werbeprospekte und Kaufhauskataloge werden immer gesucht. Den Ehrgeiz, in einem großen Modejournal zu erscheinen, hat Silke nicht. „Ständig Diät halten – furchtbar! Ich werde lieber Sekretärin oder so."

WER DEN PFENNIG NICHT EHRT

Michael trägt Werbezeitungen aus. Einmal in der Woche flitzt er auf seinen Roller-Skates drei Stunden lang von Haus zu Haus, um die 400 Briefkästen seines Bezirks zu füttern. „Für jede Zeitung gibt es vier Pfennig. Das macht 16 Mark pro Tour", rechnet Michael vor. Sein mühsam verdientes Geld trägt Michael (16) sofort zur Sparkasse: „Mit 18 will ich mir ein Auto kaufen." Eine große Auswahl an Jobs gibt es in der kleinen Stadt, wo Michael wohnt und zur Schule geht, nicht: „In den Ferien hast du die Wahl zwischen Baustelle und Bauernhof . . . "

3
1 How often does Michael work?

2 How long does the job take him?

3 What is his job?

4 Where does he go when he has been paid?

5 What does he want the money for?

6 What sort of jobs are easiest to get in Michael's area?

10 BASIC Writing

1 Write a card to your penfriend thanking him/ her for his/her postcard. Tell him/her:

- You are also going skiing next week.

- You are going to Austria with the school.

- You hope there will be plenty of snow.

- You are looking forward to it – it is your first flight.

- You'll send a card from St Anton.

2 Your penfriend's aunt owns a small business. She will give you a part-time job next summer, but she wants you to make a formal application, including a handwritten CV (Lebenslauf). Thorsten has sent you a copy of his so you can see what is required. Read it carefully, then write your own Lebenslauf.

Lebenslauf

Name :	Thorsten Krieger
Geburtsdatum:	31. Oktober 1971
Geburtsort :	Bochum
Eltern :	Michael Krieger, Koch
	Manuela Krieger, Hausfrau
Geschwister :	keine
Schulausbildung:	1977 – 81 Grundschule in Bochum
	1982 – 87 Konrad – Adenauer Realschule
Schulabschluß:	Realschulabschluß im Sommer 88
Lieblingsfächer:	Chemie, Werken und Sport
Hobbys:	Fotografieren, Gitarre spielen
Berufswunsch:	Mechaniker

Bochum, den 7.3.88

Thorsten Krieger

1 You have just been offered a job as a sales assistant in a store in town, starting on August 1st. Write a letter to your Swiss penfriend explaining why you're so pleased to get this offer, even though you'll have to cancel your trip to Switzerland. Tell your friend what you will be doing (e.g. hours, pay, how you'll get there, what you have to wear, which department you hope to work in etc).

Exchange Visit: Summer 1989

Dates : either July 16-23 or Aug. 20-27
Accommodation : In homes of 31 band members
Concerts : 1. In pedestrian precinct
(if wet - : in sports centre)
2. St. James' Church, Thursday evening
3. Joint concert with our band , hall of Isaac Newton School, last evening
Day Trip : Not fixed (suggest 2 suitable destinations)
½ day Trip : To be arranged (give a few examples)
Entertainment : Reception in Town Hall
Disco on last evening after final concert
Cost : Fares plus pocket money
Reply : By end of month, if possible.

2 Your local twinning committee has discovered that both towns have brass bands, and is suggesting an exchange visit. The leader of your local band wants to send an official invitation to the German bandleader. He has asked you to put this information into German.

3 Write a letter (about 100 words) to Herr and Frau Goldack, owners of the Blumenwiese campsite.

– Ask if they have any part-time jobs available – you noticed British and American students when you were on holiday there last summer.

– Give your age and details of any jobs you've done.

– Say that you are prepared to try almost anything – you could help in the snack-bar, the office or the shop, you could clean the washrooms and showers.

– Say that you are prepared to live in your own small tent on the site.

– Explain that you are hoping to improve your German because you would eventually like to study it.

Acknowledgements

Cartoons: Ainslie Macleod

Photographs: Margaret Wightman

Sources of other illustrations:
Claus Bredenbrock, Zechen-Magazin, c/o Zeche Bochum, Prinz-Regent-Str. 50–60, 4630 Bochum p11; **Milka** p18; **Schneider Schulfüller** p18; **Rundblick Garbsen** p19, 92; **Tourist-Hotel-Nord** p24; **Oltner Tagblatt** p26; **Städt, Nahverkehr Berlin** p26; **Münchener Verkehrs- und Tarifverbund** p27; **Verband Deutscher Mitfahrzentralen** p28 (*Fahr mit-Spar Sprit*); **Deutsche Bundesbahn** p26, 28, 29, 47, 57, 66; **Blickpunkt, Zeitung der Deutschen Bundesbahn** p29 (*Reisetip*); **Franz Schneider Verlag** p29; **Dextro Energen** p33; **Schmorl und Seefeld** p38; **Skorpion Jugendmagazin** p38; **Kaufring** p39; **Verkehrsverein Hildesheim** p45 (restaurant ad.); **Fremdenverkehrsamt München** p46, 47, 58, 77; **Rugenberger Mühle** p48; **Pfanni-Werke** p48;

Verkehrsverein Celle p49; **Musikinstrumente-Museum Goslar** p56; **Deutsches Reisebüro GMBH** p58 (*Camping-Spass*); **Gib acht-Taschenbuch 1987,** Universum Verlagsanstalt, Wiesbaden p59 (youth hostel art.); **Berliner Bären-Stadtrundfahrt** p59 (*Potsdam*); **Sindelfinger Zeitung** p58 (*Wärmster Tag des Jahres*); **Toto/Lotto** p62; **Staatstheater Stuttgart** p64; **Auto-Kino Kirchhorst** p66; **Turngemeinde 1860 Münden** p69 (*Mündener Citylauf*); **Deutsche Bundespost** p76, 77; **Deutsche Verkehrs-Kredit-Bank** p77; **GZS Gesellschaft für Zahlungssysteme** p77 (*Eurocard*); **Freiwillige Feuerwehr Kempten/Allgäu** (*Notruf 112*) p84

Every effort has been made to locate and contact the source of each illustration. We will be pleased to rectify any omissions in future printings.